We hope you have ~~ ~~~~~~~
forward to hearing
photos. With love
Lucas, Oscar, Geo
Lily, Holly, Katie, ~~ ~~~~~~~ Elena,
Nathaniel, Nicole, George H xxxxxxxxxxxxx

Vietnam

Front cover: Junk ships in Halong Bay
Below: Tam Coc

Imperial Tombs The mausoleum of Emperor Dong Khanh is just one of several grand tombs near the former capital, Hue (page 55)

Cham Towers The most striking and puzzling Cham monuments are the famous brick temples (page 65)

Ho Chi Minh City Elegant French colonial architecture gives the city centre a distinguished air (page 72)

Sa Pa See the beautiful scenery and visit the lively market in this colourful hill town (page 46)

Hoi An Chinese merchants built ornate assembly halls in this historic trading town (page 60)

Hanoi Its bustling and picturesque Old Quarter dates back to the 13th century (page 28)

Cu Chi The claustrophobic tunnels are a vivid reminder of the war (page 81)

Halong Bay Thousands of craggy islands make a boat excursion in the bay a truly memorable experience (page 44)

Cao Dai Temple This colourful temple near Tay Ninh is the headquarters of an idiosyncratic religion (page 83)

Water puppetry An art form unique to Vietnam (pages 33, 95)

A PERFECT TOUR

Day 1–3 Hanoi

Start the day in the northern capital by taking in the architecture and atmosphere around Hoan Kiem Lake and the labyrinthine streets of the Old Quarter, admiring the French colonial heritage and visiting several museums. The next day, explore the legacy of Ho Chi Minh, whose embalmed remains are in the monumental Mausoleum. Finish at the 'Hanoi Hilton,' the infamous wartime prison. On day three, head to the western suburbs, stopping at the Temple of Literature and the Ethnology Museum. Enjoy lunch at Restaurant Bobby Chinn, then journey east for a cruise around dramatic Halong Bay.

Day 4 Halong Bay

Stop off at Cat Ba Island and visit the floating villages and caves in the countless karst islands. Take a swim off the boat and then return to Hanoi for the evening.

Day 5 Hue

After a morning flight to Hue, tour the Imperial Citadel and visit the tombs of the Nguyen Kings. Enjoy an evening cruise on the Perfume River.

Day 6 Hoi An

Stroll through the Unesco World Heritage town, exploring the shops, temples, ancient houses and cafés along the river.

Day 7 My Son

Take a morning tour of the ancient Champa holy city of My Son. Do some last-minute shopping and enjoy lunch in Hoi An, then take the evening train to Nha Trang.

OF VIETNAM

Day 9–10 Dalat

Take a morning bus to the hill resort of Dalat and check into the historic Dalat Palace Hotel. Browse the central market, then walk around the lake, taking in the old French colonial architecture. On day two, tour the outlying minority villages and the many waterfalls, then back to town for a gondola ride and visit some of the local temples.

Day 14 Mekong Delta

Spend the day in Vinh Long visiting floating markets, island villages and orchards. Be sure to sample the exotic produce and fresh fish. Take a night bus back to Ho Chi Minh City.

Day 11–12 HCMC

Take a shopping spree along Dong Khoi street, stopping to see architectural gems like the Opera House, People's Committee Building, Post Office and Notre Dame Cathedral. On day two, soak up some history at the Reunification Palace, War Remnants Museum and have afternoon tea at the Continental Hotel.

Day 13 Cu Chi Tunnels and Cao Dai Temple

Take a tour of the infamous Cu Chi Tunnels and then drive further west to the Cao Dai Temple to see Vietnam's flamboyant indigenous cult. Return to HCMC for a night bus to the Mekong Delta.

Day 8 Nha Trang

Go snorkeling in the reefs, visit the offshore islands and the Underwater World Aquarium at Vinpearl Land… or just lounge on the beach all day.

CONTENTS

INTRODUCTION

For over 2,000 years Vietnam's development as a nation has been marked by the proximity of China. No country in Southeast Asia is culturally closer to China than Vietnam, and no other country in the region has spent so long fighting off Chinese domination – often at a terrible cost in lives, economic development and political compromise.

Perhaps because of the long years of rivalry, as well as its gradual conquest of the Champa Kingdom (an ancient rival to the south), Vietnam has developed a powerful sense of national identity, possessing a unique cultural heritage that is both strongly Sinicised and also distinctively Southeast Asian.

The Vietnamese have a modern slogan: *Vietnam is a country, not a war*. But for 30 years after World War II, Vietnam was almost synonymous with war, first with the French and later with the Americans. Vestiges of war remain in the bomb craters, abandoned military hardware and labyrinths of tunnels where entire villages endured the fighting. Today the craters have been converted into fishponds, the tunnels turned into a tourist attraction.

Looking westwards to their near neighbours in Thailand, the Vietnamese see the benefits that international tourism can bring (notably hard currency from abroad) but they also worry about the associated problems – loose morals, drugs, antisocial behaviour, Aids and, underlying it all, the threat of open debate, a free press and genuine opposition.

Still, in the roughly 15 years since Vietnam first began to open up to the outside world, great changes have been made. Standards of accommodation have risen dramatically,

Kenh Ga village, near Ninh Binh

Harvesting rice

thousands of new restaurants have opened, communications have improved and most of the country is now accessible. Still more importantly, as the regime has relaxed so have the Vietnamese people. Once characterised by a certain shyness or insecurity which sometimes manifested itself in a cool or reserved manner, the Vietnamese are now amazingly open, friendly and eager to meet foreign travellers.

The Country and its Climate

The Socialist Republic of Vietnam encompasses 329,566 sq km (127,245 sq miles) – slightly larger than the United Kingdom and Ireland added together. The country is long – over 1,600km (1,000 miles) from north to south – and narrow, being as thin as 50km (32 miles) wide in the centre. The northernmost point lies just below the Tropic of Cancer, its southern extreme just above latitude 8°N, placing it squarely in the tropics. It shares land borders with China to the north and Laos and Cambodia to the west. In addition, Vietnam has a 3,450km (2,156-mile) coastline along the South China Sea in the east. The capital, Hanoi, is located in the heart of the Red River Valley, in the north of the country. The largest city – named Saigon until 1975, and now Ho Chi Minh City – dominates the fertile Mekong Delta in the south.

Vietnam's long, narrow shape and location in the Southeast Asian monsoon zone gives rise to a complex climate that varies considerably from north to south. In the north, the winter from November to April is relatively cold and humid, and temperatures may fall as low as freezing point in the mountains around Sapa. Summer, between May and October, brings higher temperatures, heavy rain and sometimes typhoons. Both the north and centre experience their hottest months during June, July and August.

Southern Vietnam's climate is more Southeast Asian, with a relatively dry season from November to April, a hot season from February to April, when temperatures may reach 35°C (95°F), and heavy rains between May and October. During this period humidity rises to between 80 and 100 percent, and conditions can be sticky and uncomfortable.

Population and Language

About 86 percent of the people are ethnic Viets, also known as Kinh. They are probably descended from a number of diverse ethnic groups, the most important elements among which are Sinitic and Malayo-Polynesian. The remaining 14 percent of the population are divided among more than 50 ethnic groups.

Vietnam's 1 million Chinese constitute the most important ethnic minority. Nearly all are Hoa, or Chinese who are naturalised Vietnamese citizens. They live mostly in the south, in Ho Chi Minh City (especially

Traditional Cham costume at the Po Nagar Cham Towers

Cholon) and in the Mekong Delta. The ancestors of the Hoa came principally from the southern Chinese provinces of Guangxi, Guangdong, Fujian, Zhejiang and Taiwan.

The Khmer, numbering nearly a million too and living mainly in the Mekong Delta, are ethnically identical to the Khmers of Cambodia and practise Theravada Buddhism. Ethnic minorities in the mountains of central and southern Vietnam form another significant group. Called *Montagnards* by the French, they include Muong, E De, Jarai, Ba Na and Sedang living in the Central Highlands. Numbering around 750,000, they have long resisted Viet influence and remain culturally distinct to the present day.

The Cham inhabit the Phan Rang and Phan Thiet regions, as well as parts of the Mekong Delta. Once masters of the central coast, they now number fewer than 150,000. The coastal Cham are predominantly Hindu, while those of the Mekong Delta are Muslim. The highlands of the north are home to numerous other minorities. These include the Tay, of which there are just over a million. Other important highland groups in this region include the Tai (close relations to the various Tai-speaking groups of Laos, Thailand and China's Yunnan Province), the Hmong and the Nung.

The national language is Vietnamese, a complex fusion of Mon-Khmer, Tai and Chinese elements. It's not an easy language for the visitor to learn, though it is easy (and sensible) to acquire some elementary vocabulary to cover basic courtesies

Christian converts

Thanks to the efforts of Jesuit missionaries from France, as well as Protestant missionaries from the US and Canada, Vietnam has an estimated 8 million Christians (the second-largest population in Southeast Asia). Protestants still face violent government persecution in rural areas while Catholic groups continue to protest for the return of confiscated land.

as well as food and travel-related terms. Fortunately, the script is Romanised, so place names and menus are more readily decipherable than in neighbouring Laos and Cambodia. English is becoming widespread, especially among the young, while older people often still retain French as a second language.

Religion and Culture

Most Vietnamese consider themselves Buddhists, but are followers of the Mahayana doctrine, as taught in China, rather than the Theravada Buddhism of nearby Thailand, Laos and Cambodia. Traditional Vietnamese values respect

A Buddhist temple near Hue

and closely adhere to the teachings of Confucius, while many Viets are also influenced by Taoism. Yet they believe in local spirits too, and practise a distinctly Southeast Asian form of spirit worship.

Vietnam's unique and complex cultural identity is in some ways paralleled by the geography of the country. The closer to China, the more Sinicised the land and its people seem. Conversely, in the centre and especially the south there is a much more Southeast Asian feel. This is apparent, to some degree, in the country's historical monuments. Hanoi is without doubt the country's major historic destination and owes much to Chinese culture and influence – its very name is derived from the Chinese *he nei*, or 'within the waters'. Traditional Vietnamese culture, such as water puppetry, music and dance, is best viewed in the Red River Delta, the ancestral homeland of the Viet people.

Further south the former Imperial City of Hue also owes a lot to Chinese cultural influences. Here, the Nguyen emperors conscientiously built their Forbidden City on the model of Beijing (albeit within a massive citadel based on the designs of the French military architect Sebastien de Vauban). Imperial ceremonies, too, were closely derived from those performed by the Chinese Emperor.

But beyond the Hai Van Pass, which divides the country south of Hue, things begin to change. This was formerly the territory of the Hinduised Kingdom of Champa, and all the way from My Son to Phan Thiet the country is studded with ancient brick towers honouring Vishnu, Shiva and other Hindu gods. There still remains a different, Southeast Asian flavour to this region which extends all the way to the Mekong Delta – home to the country's half-million ethnic Khmers. Not that Chinese influences are absent from the south: from the ancient port city of Hoi An to the teeming streets of Cholon, the culture of China has left its mark.

Landscape and Wildlife

Vietnam has more than its share of natural wonders, too. Halong Bay in the north rivals Thailand's Phang Nga Bay in the profusion of its extraordinary limestone islands and outcrops. The long central coast is dotted with fine beaches, notably at Loc Vinh, Nha Trang and Mui Ne. Here the visitor will find all kinds of water sports and some of the best seafood in the world.

The interior is dominated by the all-but-impenetrable mountains of the Annamite Cordillera and, further south, the Central Highlands. Vietnam has been regarded as one

Exploring Halong Bay

of Asia's most biologically diverse countries – an evolutionary hotspot. The Vu Quang Wildlife Reserve has even been described as 'the Galapagos of Southeast Asia', with various previously unknown flora and fauna still being discovered.

The Vietnamese government has set up various National Parks as well as marine conservation sites. Two such jewels are the Bach Ma National Park in the Central Highlands, and Cat Tien National Park in the south. Bach Ma's inhabitants include the elusive clouded leopard. Although the last mainland Javan Rhino was killed by poachers in Cat Tien in 2010, much rare wildlife remains in the park. In the early 1990s the Vietnamese government, with the help of the World Wildlife Fund (WWF), began turning its attention to the protection of marine areas, leading to the establishment of the Hon Mun Marine Park in Nha Trang. The park is now one of Vietnam's foremost snorkelling and scuba diving sites.

A BRIEF HISTORY

The early history of Vietnam, like that of all ancient countries, is lost in the mists of time and legend. What is clear beyond doubt is that the ancestors of today's Kinh (as the Vietnamese call themselves) first flourished three to four millennia ago in the fertile floodplains of southernmost China and the Red River Valley of Tonkin. The story of Vietnamese survival and their long fight for freedom and independence is one of southern territorial expansion – defending against China in the north, while systematically conquering and assimilating the kingdoms of Champa and Cambodia to the south.

Legendary Kings

Vietnamese legend has it that King De Minh, descendant of a divine Chinese ruler, married an immortal mountain fairy. The product of their union, Kinh Duong, in turn married the daughter of the Dragon Lord of the Sea. Their son, Lac Long Quan or 'Dragon Lord of Lac', is considered the first Vietnamese king. To maintain peace with their powerful neighbours, the Chinese – a theme constant throughout Viet history – Lac Long Quan married Au Co, yet another Chinese immortal, who bore him 100 sons. Subsequently Lac Long Quan's eldest son succeeded him as the first king of the Hung Dynasty.

Long-lived dynasty

According to oral tradition, the Hung Dynasty had 18 kings, each of whom ruled for 150 years. This belief alone makes any attempt at accurately dating or even verifying these events quite pointless.

Rather than viewing the Hung Dynasty as a historical fact, it should be seen as a heroic legend set in mythical terms to glorify the early establishment of the Vietnamese nation. During this time the southward territorial imperative of both the Han Chinese and the Vietnamese was established, and thereby a rivalry that has lasted for millennia.

In 258BC Thuc Pan, ruler of Au Viet, overthrew the 18th Hung king and established a new Vietnamese state called Au Lac, with its capital at Co Loa just north of present-day Hanoi. Within half a century, in 207BC, a renegade Chinese general, Trieu Da, conquered Au Lac and established power over Nam Viet, a state based in what is now Guangxi in southern China and the Red River Delta of northern Vietnam. Chinese dominion over Nam Viet was confirmed in 111BC when the heirs of Trieu Da formally

Vietnamese temples show a strong Chinese influence

submitted to the Han emperor Wu Ti, establishing Chinese rule as far south as the Hai Van Pass and making Nam Viet the Chinese province of Giao Chau.

A Thousand Years of Chinese Rule

During the 1st century Chinese attempts to Sinicise the people of Giao Chau were partly successful but provoked widespread hostility among the Vietnamese. In AD40 this resulted in the first major Viet rebellion against the Chinese, led by the Trung sisters, two Viet ladies of noble birth who proclaimed themselves joint queens of an independent Vietnam. The Trung sisters are still honoured as national heroines, but their attempt at breaking away from Chinese rule did not last. Just three years later, General Ma Vien re-established Chinese control over the territory and intensified the process of Sinification. The Vietnamese increasingly came under the Chinese spell, imitating the customs of the great northern neighbour they resented so much.

For the next nine centuries the Viets remained in thrall to the Chinese, despite a series of major rebellions. In 544 the Viet nationalist Ly Bon led a rising which achieved partial independence under the Early Ly Dynasty, but this was crushed by Chinese armies in 603. The victorious Chinese renamed the country An Nam, or 'Pacified South' – though this would prove to be wishful thinking. In 938 the Viet patriot Ngo Quyen decisively defeated the Chinese at the Battle of the Bach Dang River and reasserted Vietnamese independence after almost 1,000 years of Chinese domination. At last the Viets were free, but by this time they had become the most Sinicised people in Southeast Asia, in marked contrast to their Cham, Tai and Khmer neighbours, all of whom had fallen under the philosophic and religious influence of India.

The Vietnamese had learned at least one valuable lesson from their centuries of confrontation with China. The Chinese threat wasn't going to go away, and they had to live with their northern neighbours. They achieved this by combining fierce resistance to Chinese aggression with contrite, even humble apologies to the Dragon Throne every time the Chinese were repelled. This rather clever system was formalised in 968 when King Dinh Tien, founder of

Roads to victory

Hanoi has at least 120 street names that commemorate struggles against foreign aggression. The list includes 58 celebrating victories over Chinese imperialism, 61 marking victories over French colonialism, but just two celebrating the defeat of the USA during the Second Indochina War.

the Dinh Dynasty, reaffirmed Vietnamese independence but agreed to pay tribute to the Chinese every three years. In a word, it was a matter of face.

Vietnam Moves South

From the 11th century on, Vietnam found new ways of imitating China, the neighbour it had learned both to admire and fear. Firstly, Buddhism began to make headway as a major religion in Vietnam – though this was the Mahayana faith introduced from China, and not the Theravada system practised elsewhere in Southeast Asia. Confucianism, too, was enthusiastically adopted from the Chinese and established as the basis of state administration.

Yan Po Nagar, a Cham goddess at the Po Nagar Cham Towers

Secondly, the Vietnamese people, hemmed in by the more populous Chinese to the north and the jagged mountains of the Annamite Cordillera to the west, began to expand in the only direction open to them – southwards. From their new capital at Thanh Long, or 'Ascending Dragon' (later renamed Hanoi) the long subjugation and conquest of the ancient Hindu Kingdom of Champa was begun.

The Viets continued to hold the north with considerable success, defeating a Mongol invasion in 1279 at the Second Battle of the Bach Dang River. By the 14th century central Vietnam as far as the Hai Van Pass had been captured, with the city of Hue passing under Viet suzerainty. In 1428 yet another Chinese invasion was defeated by the national hero Le Loi. Meanwhile, to the south, Qui Nhon was seized from Champa in 1471, and the Cham Kingdom was reduced to a near-powerless rump.

By the beginning of the 16th century everything seemed to be going well for Dai Viet, the Kingdom of the Vietnamese, but new troubles were just around the corner. In 1516 the first Westerners, in the form of Portuguese seafarers, arrived in the country. Moreover, in the distant south, as Champa was subjugated, rival claimants to Hanoi's rule were emerging among the Viets themselves. In 1527 the country split in two, with the Mac (and subsequently Trinh) Lords ruling the Red River Delta region from Hanoi, while the Nguyen Lords dominated the south of the country from their capital at Hue.

By the 17th century the French had replaced the Portuguese as the predominant Westerners in Vietnam, where they paid particular attention to the centre and the south. The French introduced Catholicism, which gradually spread throughout the country, despite the best efforts of the Confucian and Buddhist establishments. As a consequence, Vietnam was to become the second most Christian country in Asia, surpassed only by the Philippines. As a corollary of this missionary effort, the French priest Alexandre de Rhodes developed the Quoc Ngu system of Romanised Vietnamese script which is still used throughout the country today.

By 1757 Vietnam settlers had bypassed the small surviving bastion of Champa between Phan Rang and Phan Thiet and had begun their conquest of the Mekong Delta, until this time under Cambodian control. The Khmer settlement of Prey Nokor was taken from the Cambodians and renamed Saigon. Finally, in the 19th century, the last vestiges of Champa were snuffed out and Vietnam assumed full control over the territories which it controls today.

The Nguyen Emperors and French Conquest

In 1802 the Lord Nguyen Anh defeated his northern rivals and established the Nguyen Dynasty (1802–1945) at Hue, where he proclaimed himself Emperor Gia Long. For the first time in Vietnam's history, power shifted south from the Red River Delta to the centre of the country. Yet the authority of the Nguyen did not remain unchallenged for long. In 1858 France seized both Danang and Saigon, laying the foundations for its colonies in Annam and Cochinchina. By 1883, supported by modern weapons and an unshakeable belief in their 'civilising mission', the French proclaimed Tonkin a colony too, and Vietnam had become a French protectorate. In 1887 this was formalised and extended with the proclamation of an Indochinese Union of Vietnam, Laos and Cambodia: French Indochina had become a reality.

A statue of Nguyen emperor Quang Trung, Qui Nhon

Predictably, the Vietnamese rejected French imperialism. A proud people who had resisted Chinese domination for two millennia were hardly likely to submit quietly to French rule. Meanwhile, in 1890 at a small hamlet in rural Vinh, Ho Chi Minh, the future leader of Vietnam's struggle for independence, was born.

In 1918 Ho travelled to Paris, and three years later joined the French Communist Party. By 1930 he had visited Moscow, become an agent of the Comintern, and formed the Indochinese Communist Party in Hong Kong. The French didn't know it yet, but the writing was already on the wall.

Ho continued to organise his compatriots for independence throughout the war years and the Japanese occupation, which ended in 1945. Of course the communists weren't the only force opposed to French colonialism – Vietnamese of all political colours wanted their freedom – but there can be no doubt the communists were the best organised.

Three Indochina Wars

Following the Japanese capitulation on 15 August 1945, events moved rapidly towards a series of three Indochina Wars. On 23 August Bao Dai, the last Nguyen Emperor, abdicated. Just 10 days later, on 2 September 1945, Ho Chi Minh declared Vietnamese independence in Hanoi.

A shrine to Ho Chi Minh in his home town near Vinh

This was unacceptable to the French, and in 1946 the First Indochina War began as France sought to reimpose colonial rule. The French fared badly, and in 1954

The Viet Minh cemetery at Dien Bien Phu

suffered a crushing defeat at the hands of Ho Chi Minh's greatest general, Vo Nguyen Giap, at Dien Bien Phu. Vietnam was subsequently divided at the 17th parallel, theoretically pending elections. North Vietnam, with its capital at Hanoi, was ruled by a communist regime under Ho Chi Minh. South Vietnam, with its capital at Saigon, was ruled by a pro-Western, Catholic strongman, Ngo Dinh Diem. In 1955 Diem refused to hold elections and, backed by Hanoi, Viet Minh forces began armed attacks in the south. This event led to the start of the Second Indochina War – known to the Vietnamese as the 'American War', which would ravage the country for almost 20 years. In a misconceived attempt to contain communism, the United States first sent advisers to assist the southern regime in 1960. By 1965 the USAF had started regular bombing of the north, and US combat troops had landed at Danang in the south. By 1968 US troop strength had risen to more than half a million men, but that year's Tet Offensive by the Viet

Cong sapped Washington's will to fight, and in 1973 the last US combat troops were withdrawn. Within two years, in April 1975, the North Vietnamese Army (NVA) had captured Saigon and Vietnam was once again unified by force.

Hanoi's victory led to the proclamation of the Socialist Republic of Vietnam. Supporters of the US were sent to concentration camps and a command economy was implemented for more than a decade. Most Vietnamese suffered dire poverty and political oppression. This was compounded by the Third Indochina War (1978–79), when Vietnam invaded Cambodia to oust the murderous Khmer Rouge regime and was in turn invaded as a 'lesson' by Communist China.

Economic Growth

In 1986, Communist Party leadership launched the country on an ambitious programme of social and economic reform called doi moi. Collectivisation of land was rolled back, and a new emphasis was placed on the productivity and personal rights of the people. Consequently, agricultural production increased and Vietnam became a major rice exporter. Most impressively, the economy grew at an average rate of greater than 7 percent for a decade, until inflation hit in 2008 and economic growth began to drop. Despite these developments, political controls remain strict, and individual rights of expression remain limited. Severe crackdowns have resulted in riots in 2010 and 2011, widespread censorship of the internet and imprisonment of foreign pro-democracy activists.

Radish harvest in the hills outside Dalat

Historical Landmarks

258BC Vietnamese state called Au Lac established near present Hanoi.
207BC Chinese conquer Au Lac
AD40 Rebellion of the Trung Sisters
938 Battle at Bach Dang ends 1,000 years of Chinese domination.
1005 Buddhism established as major religion of Vietnam.
1471 Champa suffers crushing military defeat by Vietnam.
1516 Portuguese seafarers are first Westerners to arrive in Vietnam.
1539–1778 Trinh Lords dominate the north; Nguyen Lords rule the south.
1802–19 Emperor Gia Long establishes Nguyen dynasty at Hue.
1858 French forces seize Danang and Saigon.
1883 France establishes protectorate over Vietnam.
1940 Japan occupies Vietnam, leaving French administration intact.
1945 Japan defeated; Ho Chi Minh declares independence.
1946 First Indochina War begins.
1954 French defeated, Vietnam divided at 17th parallel.
1955 Second Indochina War begins; first US aid to South Vietnam.
1968 US troop strength rises to 540,000.
1969 Ho Chi Minh dies aged 79.
1973 Washington and Hanoi sign ceasefire.
1975 NVA captures Saigon. Communist victory in the south.
1976 The Socialist Republic of Vietnam is declared.
1978 Vietnam invades Cambodia in Third Indochina War.
1979 China retaliates by short invasion of northern Vietnam.
1986 Sixth Party Congress embraces *doi moi* economic reforms.
1989 Vietnamese troops leave Cambodia.
1994 US trade embargo lifted.
1995 Vietnam joins Association of Southeast Asian Nations (ASEAN).
2007 Vietnam officially joins the World Trade Organisation.
2008 Massive inflation causes economic uncertainty.
2009 Vietnam blocks Facebook; arrests of bloggers and journalists.
2012 US citizen Nguyen Quoc Quan arrested as political prisoner. Tensions rise in Spratly Islands dispute with China.

WHERE TO GO

Travel in Vietnam is not always convenient. After decades of war and with an economy that was subsequently throttled, the country's infrastructure – or lack of it – can test the most hardened traveller's patience. But Vietnam is one of those destinations where the inconveniences pale beside the remarkable, and where the beauty of its culture seduces all. The residue of warfare is now part of the country's tourism attractions, whether for the Cu Chi tunnels outside of the former Saigon or the rusting heaps at a Hanoi war museum. However, beyond the memories of war the bright tropical sun illuminates a coastline of serene, white-sand beaches and clear, blue waters, and mists veil forested mountains that are alive with exotic animals.

Northern Vietnam is anchored by Hanoi, an ancient city established more than 1,000 years ago. The old villas and façades of the French colonial era give the city an ambience not found anywhere else in Asia. Beyond Hanoi, the provinces of the vast Red River Delta reflect the traditional agricultural culture on which the economy is based. And beyond the delta's plains, the cooler mountain regions, populated by hill tribes, ascend towards the west and Laos and north towards China.

Southwards, following the historical movement of the Viet people, the traveller finds a chain of coastal provinces washed by the South China Sea. In the old imperial city of Hue, an overwhelming sense of the past pervades the streets. The antiquities don't end here. In the southern lands of the ancient kingdom of Champa are decaying sanctuaries, temples and towers that testify to its conquest by the Viet people from the north. Then there is the city of Ho Chi Minh. Often still

Scenery near Sa Pa in the far north

called Saigon, it is reviving its long-time image as the clichéd hustling-and-bustling city of people on the make and on the go. Where Hanoi is quiet, Ho Chi Minh is frenetic. If Hanoi is a city of earth tones, Ho Chi Minh is neon, all lit up in gaudy lights. The country has moved far beyond a century of foreign domination and war, and the traveller will find that Vietnam is a land of the ascending dragon and a place finally at peace.

HANOI

Hanoi ❶ is quite simply the most charming and traditional capital city in Southeast Asia. Although it was surprisingly little damaged by bombing during the Second Indochina War,

Hanoi, the Northern Capital

The area around Hanoi – the name means 'within the waters' after the city's close relationship with the Red River and numerous surrounding lakes – has been the site of Vietnam's capital for most of the last 2,000 years. In the 3rd century BC King Thuc Pan established the earliest Vietnamese capital at the citadel of Co Loa just north of the present-day city. Over 1,000 years later, when the Chinese were driven out and independence restored, General Ngo Quyen symbolically chose Hanoi as the site of the new Viet nation.

Subsequently in 1802 the first Nguyen Emperor, Gia Long, transferred the capital to Hue, but this was a short-lived move. In 1902 France established Hanoi as the capital not just of Vietnam, but of all French Indochina. In 1954 the city became the capital of the communist north, and in 1975, following the defeat of the non-communist south, it was proclaimed capital of the consolidated Socialist Republic of Vietnam. While Ho Chi Minh City has unquestionably become the centre of commerce and modern pop culture, Hanoi is Vietnam's political capital and traditional cultural centre.

Hanoi is home to Vietnam's Presidential Palace

when the country first began to open up after the communist seizure of power, years of political isolation and failed socialist economics had reduced the city to shabby penury. Today all that is changing, and things continue to improve. Modern Hanoi is a mix of the very old and the very new, from the tiny lanes of the Old Quarter to the upmarket neighbourhoods of My Dinh. Hanoi has an entrancing mix of indigenous Sino-Vietnamese and French colonial architecture. The people here are engaging, the food is excellent and varied, and even the entertainment scene is livening up. Hanoi is also a city of culture *par excellence*, with many museums and art galleries, and a thriving artistic scene.

Hanoi may be broadly divided into three districts – the **Old Quarter**, between the Song Hong (Red River) and the northern rim of Hoan Kiem Lake, **Central Hanoi** around the former French Quarter to the south of Hoan Kiem, and **Western Hanoi**, home to the Presidential Palace and Ho Chi Minh's

Mausoleum. Beyond lie the city's sprawling suburbs.

The Old Quarter

Hanoi's historic **Old Quarter** is also known as **Ba Muoi Sau Pho Phuong**, 'The 36 Streets'. This area, which is almost entirely devoted to commerce, dates back seven centuries to the time when a group of 36 guilds established themselves in the area, each on a particular street. Today many of the original street names survive. Examples include **Hang Ma** (Paper Street), **Hang Bac** (Silver Street), **Hang Thiec** (Tin Street) and **Hang Chieu** (Mat Street) – of these only Hang Bac still continues in its original craft, specialising in the sale of jewellery.

Trader in the Old Quarter

The best way to see the Old Quarter is on foot, seeking out the most lively or fascinating sights, one of which is the lively **Dong Xuan Market Ⓐ**. Long the largest market in Hanoi, Dong Xuan was built in 1889. Sadly the old market burned down in 1994, but it has since been rebuilt and retains its original facade. Of particular note are the traditional **tube houses**, long, narrow commercial buildings designed to combine shop front, storage space and living quarters, which are extremely narrow and deep. Designed in this fashion six centuries ago to minimise a swingeing government tax on shop frontage, today the best examples are found in Hanoi and the central port of

Hoi An. The most noteworthy 'tube' house is at **No 87 Ma May** (Rattan Street). A former Communal House, it has now been beautifully restored to its original condition, and is open to the public (daily 8am–5pm; charge).

While chiefly important as an area of commerce, the Old Quarter also has several important historic monuments. These include, on the eastern side of the quarter, **Cua O Quan Chuong B** (Gate of the Commander of the Garrison). This was built in 1749 and is now the sole surviving fortified gateway in Old Hanoi. Close by is **Den Bach Ma C** (White Horse Temple; daily 8am–5pm). Established more than 1,100 years ago to commemorate the spirit of a white horse that is believed to protect the Old City, the present structure dates around the 18th century.

Central Hanoi

Ho Hoan Kiem D (Hoan Kiem Lake), which means 'Lake of the Restored Sword', represents the historic heart of Old Hanoi. It was here that the revered national hero Le Loi was given a magic sword by a divine turtle that rose from the depth of the lake. After 10 years of warfare, Le Loi, armed with this magic sword, led an uprising that succeeded in driving out the hated Chinese. Legend has it that a grateful Le Loi, by now enthroned as the Emperor Le Thai Tho, returned the sword to the divine turtle, which is still believed to guard the sacred weapon beneath the waters of the lake. In the middle of the lake a small

Thap Rua stands on an islet in the middle of the lake

Elegant The Huc (Sunrise Bridge) on Ho Koan Kiem

pagoda, **Thap Rua** (Tortoise Tower), standing on a small islet, commemorates these events.

Today Ho Hoan Kiem remains a tranquil retreat from the hustle and bustle of the Old City to the north and the more upmarket boulevards of Downtown Hanoi to the south. At the northeastern corner of the lake stands the elegant **Writing Brush Pillar**, a tall stone column in the shape of a traditional brush pen engraved with Chinese characters which proclaim 'writing on a blue sky'. It was erected by the 19th-century scholar Nguyen Van Sieu. Close by, the graceful, red-lacquered arch of **The Huc** (Sunrise Bridge), built in 1885, leads to a small island and to **Den Ngoc Son** (Temple of the Jade Mound; daily 8am–5pm; charge). Founded in the 14th century, this splendid building was originally a Confucian temple. Between the 16th and 18th centuries it served as a pavilion for the Trinh Lords of

Hanoi, while in the 19th century it was re-established as a Buddhist temple.

Nearby, on the eastern side of Pho Dinh Tien Hoang, is a fine old temple that has been converted to serve as an art gallery. Elsewhere the shop fronts along the northern and western sides of Hoa Koan Kiem house many galleries selling some really fine paintings – as well as, inevitably, some kitsch. This is a good area to stroll and shop, especially as there are plenty of small restaurants and cafés where iced beer and excellent Vietnamese coffee are available.

A real must for visitors to Hanoi is *mua roi nuoc*, or water puppetry, popularly performed by the **Thang Long Water Puppet Theatre** ❺ (Mon–Sat 5.15pm, 6.30pm and 8pm, Sun 9.30am; charge; www.thanglongwaterpuppet.org) at the Kim Dong Theatre on 57 Dinh Tien Hoang – not far from the eastern end of The Huc Bridge. The art of water-puppetry is unique to Vietnam and is believed to have originated in the Red River Delta more than 1,000 years ago. The puppets are carved from a hard, water-resistant wood to represent both characters from rural lifestyles, such as farmers and bullocks, and mythical creatures like dragons and phoenixes. The puppeteers stand concealed, waist-deep in water, and use a complex system of ropes and pulleys to manipulate their charges with remarkable skill, while a traditional orchestra plays accompanying music.

Water puppets

To the east a path winds beneath shady trees, and to the west of the lake groups of old men play chess, and mixed groups of men and women practise *tai chi*. Off Hang Trong, a road leading west from the lake, is Pho Nha Tho (Church Street), on which stands the neo-Gothic **St Joseph's Cathedral** **F** (daily 5am–noon, 2–7pm).

South of the lake lies the commercial heart of Hanoi, an area originally built by the French, which is rapidly being modernised. Although it is dominated by broad, east–west boulevards and shopfronts, the small **Chua Quan Su** (Ambassador's Pagoda) is tucked away on a side street at 73 Quan Su. Unfortunately little of the original 17th-century structure survives, and what we see today dates mainly from the 1930s. Once a lodging for ambassadors from neighbouring Buddhist countries, it remains an active Buddhist centre.

Dominating the central Hanoi skyline on Pho Hoa Lo, a high-rise tower marks the former site of **Hoa Lo** **G**, a prison built by the French in 1896, in which thousands of Vietnamese political prisoners were incarcerated during the colonial period. Today it is better known to most Western visitors as the '**Hanoi Hilton**', the nickname it was given by US prisoners of war held here during the Second Indochina War. In the mid-1990s the prison was demolished to make way for a shopping mall and hotel complex, but a small part of the prison was preserved as a museum exhibiting a few cells, stocks and a guillotine.

Playing football outside St Joseph's Cathedral

Further east on busy Ngo Quyen the former **Residence of the Governor of Tonkin** is an elegant colonial building dating from 1918. Nearby, at the eastern end of Pho Trang Thi, the restored **Opera House** **H**

Tran Quoc Pagoda, one of the oldest temples in Vietnam

(Nha Hat Lon) now functions as a municipal theatre. This magnificent building, styled after the neo-baroque Paris Opera, was regarded as the most sophisticated expression of French culture in all Indochina.

East of the Opera House, by the Red River embankment, a few of the museums include the **Bao Tang Cach Mang** ❶ (Museum of Vietnamese Revolution; Tue–Sun 8–11.45am, 1.30–4.15pm; charge) and the **Bao Tang Lich Su Viet Nam** ❷ (National Museum of Vietnamese History; www.nmvnh.com.vn; Tue–Sun 8–11.30am, 1.30–4.30pm; charge). This last, founded in the 1930s, houses an impressive collection of artefacts.

Western Hanoi

The delightful **Chua Tran Quoc** ❸ (Tran Quoc Pagoda; daily 7–11.30am, 1.30–6.30pm; free) is picturesquely situated on an island west of the causeway separating Truc Bach Lake from the much larger Ho Tay (West Lake). It's one of

Vietnam's oldest temples, dating back to the 6th-century Early Ly Dynasty.

Further south along Duong Hung Vuong, next to the **Gong Vien Bach Thao** ⓛ, (Hanoi Botanical Gardens; daily 7am–10pm; free) is the **Phu Chu Tich** ⓜ (Presidential Palace). This particularly fine example of French colonial architecture was built in 1906 as the Palace of the Governor General of Indochina. Although it is closed to the public, it's possible to walk through the palace grounds along a clearly marked route to visit **Nha San Bac Ho** (Ho Chi Minh's House; daily except Mon and Fri 7.30–11.30am; charge), an unassuming residence on stilts where Ho spent the last decade of his

Vietnamese Temple Architecture

A Vietnamese pagoda consists of several rooms. At the front are doors that are opened only for major religious festivals. Behind these doors lie a front hall, a central hall and the main altar room, usually arranged in ascending levels. Behind the temple, or to the side, are living quarters for monks or nuns. There will also usually be one or more subsidiary altar rooms specifically dedicated to the rites of ancestor worship, where funerary tablets and pictures of deceased monks and relatives are displayed.

Vietnamese temples are generally distinguished by their lavish use of dragon motifs. These are not the dangerous creatures of Western mythology, but the noble and beneficial dragons of imperial Chinese tradition. Look for them outside, on the eaves and the apex of main roofs; inside they may be twined around supporting pillars, holding up altars, and guarding doorways. Other decorative images to look for include Buddhist swastika motifs and the yin-yang icon of Taoism symbolising the duality, or male and female elements of existence. Chinese characters, too, although long abandoned by modern written Vietnamese, remain an essential part of the Viet spirit world.

life. The atmosphere is distinctly ascetic, with a small garden and pond. On the first floor the bedroom and study are preserved as Ho left them, with a few simple possessions.

Immediately to the south, the austere **Lang Chu Tich Ho Chi Minh** (Ho Chi Minh Mausoleum; Tue–Thur, Sat–Sun 8–11am; charge) faces the **National Assembly** across **Ba Dinh Square**. It was here that Ho read the Vietnamese Declaration of Independence on 2 September 1945, and it was here that he was entombed after his death on 2 September 1969, despite his wish to be cremated and

Keeping guard outside the Ho Chi Minh Mausoleum

scattered across the country. The mausoleum, built in Stalinist style and modelled on the Mausoleum of Lenin in Red Square, was completed in 1975 using marble, granite and rare woods brought from all over Vietnam. Visitors may enter and briefly view Ho's embalmed body. Respectful dress is a requirement, and photography is strictly prohibited.

A short distance to the south is the celebrated **Chua Mot Cot** (One Pillar Pagoda), a diminutive but elegant structure erected by King Ly Thai Tong in the 11th century. The single column on which the pagoda rests rises from a tranquil lotus-filled pond. The pipal (bo tree) growing by the temple was planted by President Nehru of India during a state visit in 1958 and is said to be an offshoot of the tree under which the Buddha attained enlightenment. The attractive facade of the nearby **Dien Huu Pagoda** (daily 6–11am, 2–6pm) opens on to a quiet garden courtyard. Many Vietnamese visitors come for the acupuncture treatment with which the temple is associated.

Dominating both pagodas is the **Bao Tang Ho Chi Minh** Ⓟ (Ho Chi Minh Museum; Tue–Thur and Sat 8–11.30am, 2–6pm; charge); it opened on 19 May 1990, the 100th anniversary of Ho's birth. Exhibits portray aspects of Ho's life and the course of the Vietnamese Revolution.

The amazing One Pillar Pagoda dates from the 11th century

On Dien Bien Phu, a boulevard of shady trees and elegant colonial buildings, you will find the **Bao Tang Lich Su Quan Su** Ⓠ (Military History Museum; Tue–Thur and Sat–Sun 8–11.30am, 1–4.30pm; charge). Well-documented displays of Vietnamese military history feature wars against the Chinese, French and Americans. The museum courtyard delimits the southwest corner of the **Citadel**, formerly the centre of administration in pre-colonial times and today a restricted military area. **Cot Co**, or the Flag Tower, which is the most interesting surviving feature of the Citadel, is open to the public and well worth the climb for the magnificent views over the city to the Song Hong and the historic **Long Bien Bridge**.

Nearby Nguyen Thai Hoc is home to the **Bao Tang My Thuat** ⓡ (Fine Arts Museum; Tue–Sun 8.30am–5pm; charge) providing interesting exhibitions of art history from the Dong Son period, through the Kingdom of Champa and pre-colonial Vietnamese dynasties, to contemporary times. At the far west side of Hanoi is the **Bao Tang Dan Toc Hoc Viet Nam** (Vietnam Museum of Ethnology; Nguyen Van Huyen Road; Tue–Sun 8.30am–5.30pm; charge)

Inside the Ho Chi Minh Museum

Van Mieu

South of Nguyen Thai Hoc is the much smaller Van Mieu Road leading to **Van Mieu** ⓢ (Temple of Literature; daily 8am–5pm; charge) on Pho Quoc Tu Giam Street. Founded in 1070 by King Ly Thanh Tong, the temple was originally dedicated both to Confucius and to Chu Cong, a Chinese sage who conceived some of the teachings that Confucius developed five centuries later. The tradition of Confucian education flourished at Van Mieu, and in 1484 the first stele bearing the names of doctoral graduates was erected. The last examinations to be conducted here were in 1915.

Entry to the temple complex is through **Van Mieu Gate**. The layout, based on that of the temple at Qufu in China where Confucius was born, consists of a succession of five walled courtyards. The first two, joined by **Dai Trung Mon** (Great Middle Gate), are carefully maintained gardens where

Van Mieu, the Temple of Literature

locals come to paint, read or just talk. The third courtyard is reached via **Khue Van Cac** (Pavilion of the Constellation of Literature), a fine double-roofed gateway built in 1805. Here the visitor will find the **Garden of Stelae**, containing 82 stone memorials mounted on the backs of tortoises, each listing the names and brief biographical details of graduates of Van Mieu dating back to the 15th century.

Entry to the fourth courtyard (the Courtyard of the Sages), is via **Dai Thanh Mon** (Gate of the Great Synthesis). It was here, in the **Great House of Ceremonies**, that in times past the king would make offerings at the **Altar to Confucius** while new university graduates would kneel and prostrate themselves to pay respect. Behind the Great House of the Ceremonies is the **Sanctuary**, with statues of Confucius and his leading disciples including Manh Tu, better known as Mencius. The fifth and final courtyard contains the **Lieu Hanh Shrine**, dedicated to the goddess who is one of the Four Immortals honoured in Vietnamese tradition.

DAY TRIPS FROM HANOI

There are a number of worthwhile attractions in the vicinity of Hanoi, though they are scattered at all points of the compass at varying distances from the city. Travel between these places can be awkward, so it's best to stay in the capital and plan day-trips to selected destinations.

North of Hanoi

The first known independent Viet kingdom was created in 258BC when King An Duong established his capital at **Co Loa** 16km (26 miles) north of present-day Hanoi. There is little left of the original city, but a half-day trip to Co Loa Citadel is well worth the effort. An Duong built his capital within three concentric ramparts, which spiralled like the shell of a snail, and these are still just visible today. Close to the Citadel's former south gateway, a large pipal tree shades **Den My Chau**, a temple dedicated to An Duong's daughter, princess My Chau. Nearby **Den An Duong Vuong** is dedicated primarily to King An Duong, but also to the magical Golden Turtle Kim Quy. The terrace rests on six turned and lacquered pillars that support a long roof with curving eaves.

The town of **Thai Nguyen**, 76km (48 miles) north of Hanoi, is notable for its excellent **Museum of the Nationalities of Vietnam** (Tue–Sun 7–11am, 2–5.30pm; charge). If you are interested in Vietnam's many colourful minorities, a visit is well worth the journey. The exhibits include everyday artefacts, costumes, photographs and video presentations, displayed in five large rooms divided by linguistic groups. The Mon-Khmer Room, recently redesigned, is particularly fascinating. The museum is in the centre of town.

In Den My Chau, Co Loa

Dong Ky woodcarving village

East of Hanoi

The Song Hong Delta is well known for handicraft production, and several small villages within easy reach of Hanoi are traditionally associated with particular crafts. About 13km (8 miles) southeast of the capital on the left bank of the Song Hong the settlement of **Bat Trang** is renowned for its blue and white ceramics. There are around 2,000 families in Bat Trang, managing no fewer than 800 kilns. The village of **Van Phuc**, about 8km (5 miles) southwest of the capital on Route 6 to Hoa Binh, is famous for its silk production. **So**, a small village about 12km (7.5 miles) further out on the same road, is known for producing hand-made noodles. **Dong Ky** village, about 15km (9 miles) northeast of the capital on Route 1 to Bac Ninh, is celebrated for its woodcarving. Visitors are always welcome at all these craft villages, and most tour companies in Hanoi are able to arrange short tours.

South and West of Hanoi

Chua Huong ② (Perfume Pagoda; charge), established by the Trinh Lords in the 17th and 18th centuries, is set in the mountains some 60km (38 miles) southwest of Hanoi. It's possible to drive directly to Chua Huong, but the most popular way to go is by boat from Duc Khe on the Yen River. The river trip, winding through outstandingly beautiful countryside, takes around 2 hours, after which you have to walk about 4km (2.5 miles) to the temple complex.

Chua Thay (Pagoda of the Teacher; charge) is situated about 40km (25 miles) southwest of Hanoi on the shores of Long Tri Lake in Ha Tay Province. It's also known as **Thien Phuc Tu** (Heavenly Blessing Pagoda), and is dedicated to Thich Ca or Sakyamuni Buddha. To the right of the main altar stands a statue of King Ly Nhan Tong (1072–1127), during whose reign the pagoda was constructed, and to the left a statue of Tu Dao Hanh, the monk who first managed the establishment and was also a teacher and doctor to the local residents – hence the name of the pagoda. Tu Dao Hanh is said to have been a master water-puppeteer, and demonstrations of this ancient skill are given at the temple during the annual festival that takes place on the 5th to 7th days of the third lunar month.

Nearby **Chua Tay Phuong** (Western Pagoda; charge), lies some 6km (4 miles) to the west. Perched on top of a hill said to resemble a buffalo, Tay Phuong dates from the 8th century and is celebrated for its collection of more than 70 wooden statues representing both Buddhist and Confucian deities.

Approximately 100km (63 miles) south of Hanoi is **Tam Coc**, a land-bound version of Halong Bay. Brilliant hued rice fields surround the river and the karst hills are populated by wild goats. Viewed from the comfort of a sampan the effect is breathtaking.

Cuc Phuong's wildlife

120km (75 miles) southwest of Hanoi is Cuc Phuong National Park. Cuc Phuong has a total of 43 'biodiversity hotspots' within the park. Mammal species include the Delacour's langur, loris, Clouded leopard, Owston's civet, and Asian black bears. The 307 species of rare birds identified include the Silver-pheasant, Brown hornbill, and Bar-bellied pita.

A tourist cruise around dramatic Halong Bay

As you drift down the river you will pass under three, long, low-hanging tunnel caves, the largest complete with numerous beautiful rock formations. These have been bored through the limestone hills over the centuries. Nearby is **Hoa Lu**, site of the 10th century capital of the Vietnamese kingdom, Dai Co Viet.

FURTHER AFIELD FROM HANOI

Halong Bay
Heading east from Hanoi eventually leads to Bien Dong, or the East Sea, as the South China Sea is called in Vietnam. No trip to northern Vietnam would be complete without a trip to **Quang Ninh Province**, 165km (100 miles) from Hanoi. This province harbours one of the wonders of the world, with probably the most stunning scenery in Vietnam: **Vinh Ha Long ❸** (Halong Bay). The bay's tranquil beauty encompasses 1,500 sq km (560 sq miles) dotted with well over 3,000 limestone caves,

many of them not named. It is no wonder that Halong Bay was designated a Unesco World Heritage Site in 1994.

In Vietnamese *ha long* means 'descending dragon', and legend has it that Halong Bay was formed by a celestial dragon which plunged into the Gulf of Tonkin, creating thousands of limestone outcrops by lashing its tail.

The most spectacular islands and dramatic caves lie in the western part of the bay. The best way of appreciating Halong Bay is by boat, and this is best organised from Hanoi, where every tour operator arranges one- to four-day tours of the bay, and includes transfers, meals and accommodation on a boat. Unscrupulous boat owners in **Halong City** are notorious for ripping off tourists, so it's best not to do this trip on your own. Boats depart from **Bai Chay**, some 165km (102 miles) east of Hanoi by road. For those with limited time, there are one-day tours with roughly four hours cruising, but this is not worthwhile given the three-hour road journey to Bai Chay.

Boats usually visit a couple of caves en route: purchase your tickets at the Tourist Wharf. The most well-known is found on the island nearest to Halong City: **Hang Dau Go** (Grotto of the Wooden Stakes), where General Tran Hung Dao amassed hundreds of stakes prior to his 1288 victory. Other sites include **Hang Thien Cung** (Grotto of the Heavenly Palace); **Hang Sung Sot** (Surprise Grotto); and **Hang Hanh**, a 2km (11-mile) tunnel cave. Also much-visited is **Ho Ba Ham** (Three-Tunnel Lake), a shallow lagoon surrounded by limestone walls on **Dau Bo Island**.

Cat Ba Island is the largest in Halong Bay at 354 sq km (136 sq miles), and it offers spectacular, rugged landscape – forested limestone peaks, offshore coral reefs, coastal mangrove and freshwater swamps, lakes and waterfalls.

Beyond Halong Bay, unlikely limestone outcrops stud the sea northwards all the way to the Chinese frontier by way of

Ba Tu Long Bay, which several tour companies now take visitors, in search of more solitude than at Cat Ba Island.

The Northwest

Rugged northwestern Vietnam offers some of the most beautiful scenery in the whole country, as well as a chance to meet minority hill peoples with cultural identities and languages quite different from the dominant Vietnamese. The most interesting way to reach this area is via the single-line narrow-gauge track leading to Kunming, the capital of China's Yunnan Province. It's also possible to travel by bus or taxi.

There's little of interest in the border town of **Lao Cai**, not least because the People's Liberation Army dynamited the whole city in 1979 as part of China's 'lesson' to Vietnam for invading Cambodia and overthrowing the murderous Khmer Rouge regime. Today it's just a place to have a meal and spend the night before heading on into the hills. At the international frontier you can watch people crossing in and out of China (quite a few of them smugglers and human traffickers) via the busy **Coc Leu Bridge**.

The hill town of **Sa Pa ❹** is 38km (24 miles) from Lao Cai by way of a narrow road that climbs slowly into the hills. Developed in 1922 as a hill station, Sa Pa lies at an elevation of 1,600m (5,200ft) and is pleasantly cool during the hot season and decidedly cold during the winter months. Besides the beautiful scenery and cool climate, this small market town affords the visitor an opportunity to sample the temperate fruits and vegetables grown here, and to interact with the local hill peoples.

Most people living in Sa Pa town are ethnic Vietnamese, while the minorities live in small villages on the outskirts. It's possible to walk to some of these settlements, one of the most popular being the Hmong village of **Cat Cat**, just 3km (2 miles) distant. There are also Dao, Red Dao and Tay villages

Views over the rice paddies around Sa Pa

within about 12km (7 miles), but most visitors make do with Sa Pa's colourful **weekend market**. This event, which is of social as well as commercial importance to the locals, runs between noon on Saturday and noon on Sunday, with hill peoples flocking in from the surrounding villages to trade. Many women dress in leggings, embroidered skirts and jackets, heavy silver jewellery and elaborate headdresses, though increasingly it's a show for tourists to boost souvenir sales.

If you are interested in the natural wilderness and military history, then a visit to the former battlefield of **Dien Bien Phu** ❺ is certainly worthwhile. It's an 18-hour journey by road from Hanoi, but there are also three flights a week. In 1954 Vietnam's celebrated military commander General Vo Nguyen Giap successfully besieged and then reduced the French garrison occupying the valley. More than 2,000 soldiers were killed and another 11,000 taken prisoner. This decisive Vietnamese victory effectively brought the First Indochina War to an end.

The former HQ of the French commander, Colonel de Castries, has been rebuilt and some rusting French tanks and heavy artillery pieces are collected nearby. Sometimes the area is closed during ethnic unrest and government sieges.

THE CENTRE

The Vietnamese sometimes liken their country to a shoulder-pole with a pannier at either end. The panniers – that is, the Red River Delta around Hanoi and the Mekong Delta south of Ho Chi Minh City – are the most densely populated regions and tend to overshadow the 'pole'. Yet the centre has a flavour quite distinct from that of either the north or the south.

Hmong women in Sa Pa market

The city of Hue was once the imperial capital and remains the most staunchly Buddhist region in the country. Just south of Danang, Vietnam's fourth largest city, the ancient and picturesque riverine port of Hoi An has been lovingly restored. South of Danang all the way down the coast to Phan Thiet stand complexes of brick temples, silent reminders of the ancient Champa kingdom which once flourished in this area, but is now diminished to a small minority. The best beaches in Vietnam are found in this area, notably between Hoi An and Danang, at Mui Ne and Nha Trang, and Jungle Beach, a hidden gem on the Hon Heo Peninsula, north of Nha Trang. Finally, a short distance inland in the cool Central Highlands, the old French hill station of Dalat is a major tourist destination.

Hue

The former imperial city of **Hue** ❻ is one of the most significant cultural monuments in Vietnam. It is a place of sublime beauty and, despite having been badly damaged during the 1968 Tet Offensive, it remains a magical place. Renowned throughout the country for the elegance of its women and its sophisticated royal cuisine, Hue lies at the very heart of Vietnamese cultural tradition. The **Song Huong** (Perfume River) flows through the city, while the surrounding countryside is studded with royal tombs built during the time of the Nguyen Kings.

Dominating the Hue skyline is the 37m (120ft) **Cot Co** (Flag Tower), first erected in 1809. Cot Co became internationally famous on 31 January 1968, when communist forces seized Hue Citadel and ran their yellow-starred banner up its tall mast. For the next 25 days Hue suffered badly as the Americans and their South Vietnamese allies struggled to recapture the city. The damage was immense, but in 1993 Unesco declared Hue a World Heritage Site, and restoration and conservation work has since continued with considerable success.

Originally part of the Kingdom of Champa, Hue first became part of Vietnam in 1306 when King Jaya Sinhavarman III ceded it to Hanoi as dowry in a royal marriage. In 1558 the city

View of Hue's Citadel, with its large flag tower

became capital of the Nguyen rulers of south-central Vietnam. In 1802 Nguyen Anh, the last of the Nguyen Lords, defeated his rivals in Hanoi and proclaimed Hue, a former Cham stronghold, the new imperial capital – at the same time proclaiming himself Emperor Gia Long. In 1805 he strengthened his position further by ordering the building of **Kinh Thanh Ⓐ**, Hue's massive moated Citadel.

Entry to the Citadel is by way of 10 fortified gates, each of which is reached by a low, arched stone bridge across the moat. In imperial times a cannon would sound at 5am and 9pm to mark the opening and closing of the gates. The area within the Citadel comprises three enclosures, the first of which was formerly used to accommodate various royal ministries and which today constitutes a pleasant area of parks, gardens and quiet residential districts. Here may be found the **Sung Than Cong Ⓑ** (Nine Deities Cannons), kept in buildings flanking the gates on either side of the **Flag Tower**.

A second moat and defensive wall within the Citadel guard the **Hoang Thanh** (Yellow City; daily 7am–5.30pm;

Music, Ancient and Modern

Traditional Vietnamese music combines indigenous techniques thought to date back to the Dong Son period. It embraces both Chinese influences and Indian influences from the Hindu Kingdom of Champa. The resultant mix, which is technically very complex, is based on a five-note scale. Traditional Vietnamese musical groups include wind instruments, string instruments, zithers and drums, which are usually accompanied by song. An excellent place to see and hear traditional Vietnamese music is at the **Royal Theatre** in the Forbidden Purple City at Hue. Contemporary music in Vietnam has inevitably been influenced by Chinese, Thai and Western pop music. The resultant Viet Pop is known as 'Nhac Tre'.

Ngan Gate: one of 10 entrances to Hue's moated Citadel

charge), deliberately modelled on the Forbidden City in Beijing. This inner city has four gates, the chief of which is called **Cua Ngo Mon ©** (Meridian Gate, also known as the Noon Gate). This majestic structure, built during the reign of Emperor Minh Mang in 1833, is among the finest surviving examples of Nguyen architecture. The central entrance, reserved exclusively for the emperor, is flanked by smaller passages for the use of mandarins and court officials; these in turn are flanked by two much wider passages intended for the royal elephants. Above the Cua Ngo Mon rises **Five Phoenix Watchtower** where the emperor sat in state during important ceremonies.

Beyond the Ngo Mon Gate, **Kim Thuy Kieu** (Bridge of Golden Waters), leads between lotus-filled ponds to **Dien Thai Hoa ©** (Palace of Supreme Harmony). This was the throne room of the Nguyen Kings, and is the best preserved of Hue's surviving palaces. Built by Gia Long in 1805, its yellow-tiled roof is supported by 80 massive wooden columns, lacquered a deep red and decorated with imperial golden dragons.

Immediately behind the throne room, **Dai Cung Mon** (Great Golden Gate) once led through to **Tu Cam Thanh** (Forbidden Purple City). This used to be the sole preserve of the emperor, his queen, his many concubines and female palace servants. No man but the king could set foot here on pain of death – imperial sons were banished when they reached puberty, and the only non-females permitted within the inner sanctum were palace eunuchs. In imperial times the Purple City consisted of more than 60 buildings arranged around 20 courtyards, but it was seriously damaged by fire in 1947 and all but destroyed during the Tet Offensive of 1968. Restoration work, based on surviving photographs, plans and some degree of imagination, was begun in the mid-1990s and is now well under way.

Just southwest of the Forbidden Purple City is an area with numerous temples and smaller palaces. **Cuong Dien Tho** ❸ (Dien Tho Palace) was the traditional residence of various queen mothers and contains more than 20 structures, including the lovely **Truong Du Pavilion**, nestled against a small lotus pond. Completely restored, the magnificent **Hien Lam Cac** (Pavilion of Splendour), towers above the **Cuu Dinh** (Nine Dynastic Urns). The urns, cast during Minh Mang's reign, are decorated with motifs of nature

Hien Lam Cac, the Pavilion of Splendour

and daily life, dragons and historic events.

Around Hue

On the north bank of the Perfume River, about 4km (2.5 miles) southwest of the Citadel, stands the celebrated **Chua Thien Mu**  **❻** (Celestial Lady Pagoda), long considered a symbol for the City of Hue. Originally founded in 1601 by Lord Nguyen Hoang, the most striking feature of the temple is a 21m (68ft) high octagonal tower, the seven-storey **Thap Phuoc Nguyen** (Tower of the Source of Happiness), which stands on a small hillock overlook-

The Thien Mu Pagoda

ing the Perfume River. Two pavilions close by house a stone stele erected in 1715 which records the history of Buddhism in Hue, and a large bronze bell, cast in 1710, which weighs over 2,000kg (2 tons). The sound of this bell is said to reach over 10km (6 miles), and in times past could clearly be heard in Hue city.

On the south bank of the Perfume River, beyond the former French quarter, is **Dan Nam Giao ❼** (Altar of Heaven). During the years of Hue's primacy this was the most important religious centre in the country, though today there isn't a lot to see beyond a series of three raised terraces. The first, square terrace is said to represent humanity, the second, also square, to represent earth, while

Song Huong, the Perfume River, outside Hue

the third, round terrace represents heaven. Here, every three years between 1806 and 1945, the Nguyen Emperors reaffirmed the legitimacy of their rule through a series of elaborate blood sacrifices to the Emperor of Heaven.

Another imperial relic is **Ho Quyen**, the Royal Arena of the Nguyen Kings, 4km (2.5 miles) southwest of Hue near the village of Phuong Duc. Tigers, a symbol of Champa, were forced to fight elephants in this amphitheatre, and the elephant, a symbol of imperial power, was always victorious. This result was achieved in a rather unsporting fashion, by de-clawing the tiger and sewing its mouth shut before battle began. The last fight was held in 1904.

Any visit to Hue should certainly include a boat trip on the beautiful **Perfume River**. Boats are readily available for hire, either for a relaxing trip in the vicinity of Hue, or for a longer journey upstream to the tombs of Minh Mang and Gia Long.

Night journeys on the river with musical ensembles playing traditional court music can be arranged and are an enchanting experience.

The Imperial Tombs

Scattered across the countryside to the south and west of the city, the **Tombs of the Nguyen Emperors** are, together with the Citadel, Hue's greatest attraction. These seven tombs, all of which have features of outstanding architectural merit, are often strikingly different. All are open 8am–5pm and charge admission.

Lang Duc Duc ❶ is the tomb nearest to Hue, but also one of the hardest to find. Located just south of the railway line on Tan Lang Lane, it was erected in 1899. Duc Duc reigned for a mere three days in 1883. Dethroned as a result of court intrigue, he later starved to death in prison. Six years later his son, Thanh Thai (1889–1907), became emperor and erected a mausoleum for Duc Duc over the spot where he had been buried.

Lang Tu Duc ❶, built between 1864 and 1867, is perhaps the most exquisitely designed of the Nguyen tombs. About 6km (4 miles) southwest of Hue, set in the hills of Thuy Xuan district, this splendid mausoleum was built by Emperor Tu Duc (1848–83). The mausoleum is set amidst fragrant pines and frangipani trees, surrounded by tranquil ponds. It was Tu Duc's habit to recline here in the gorgeous **Xung Khiem Pavilion** composing poetry, reflecting

Khai Din's tomb is ornately decorated

Lang Tu Duc, the most beautiful of the Nguyen mausoleums

on the nature of existence, or dallying with his wives and concubines.

Lang Dong Khanh ❿, the mausoleum of Emperor Dong Khanh (1885–88), lies slightly southeast of Lang Tu Duc. His mausoleum, the smallest of the Nguyen Tombs, is in exquisite taste and unusually well preserved. The exterior of the main temple is traditionally Vietnamese, but the interior shows signs of French cultural influence notably in engravings of Napoleon and the Battle of Waterloo which hang from the red-lacquered ironwood pillars supporting the roof.

About 1.5km (1 mile) from Lang Tu Duc, south of the Perfume River, is **Lang Thieu Tri ⓚ**, the mausoleum of Emperor Thieu Tri (1841–47). It is one of the smaller tombs, lacking the usual walled gardens. The tomb itself is to the west, while to the east is a temple, almost entirely surrounded by small lakes.

Lang Khai Dinh ❶, the mausoleum of Emperor Khai Dinh (1916–25), is about 10km (6 miles) southwest of Hue. Built between 1920 and 1931, the tomb rises through a series of stairs and courtyards on the side of a low hill.

Lang Minh Mang ⓜ, the mausoleum of Emperor Minh Mang (1820–41), lies on the west bank of the Perfume River about 12km (7 miles) from Hue. The complex – which includes elegant portals, bridges, lakes and pavilions, as well as the **Sung An Temple**– is perhaps the most impressive of all the Nguyen Tombs.

Lang Gia Long ⓝ, the mausoleum of the first Nguyen Emperor Gia Long (1802–20), is also located on the left bank of the Perfume River, a 20-minute boat ride and short walk south of the Minh Mang ferry crossing. Remote from Hue and severely damaged during the Second Indochina War, this tomb is visited by relatively few people.

South of Hue

Unless you are a military buff or a veteran of the Second Indochina War, there's little to see to the immediate north of Hue. The provinces around the former Demilitarised Zone are among the poorest in Vietnam, with nothing in the way of cultural and historic sites, but a good deal to offer – at least off the beaten track – in terms of 'UXO', or unexploded ordinance. Unless entering or exiting the country by way of the Lao Bao crossing to neighbouring Laos, there is little to draw the visitor to these regions.

South of Hue is another matter. The road from Hue to Danang is among the most beautiful in the country, running past extensive lagoons with dense bird populations at **Thuy Tu** and **Cau Hai** before meeting the sea at **Lang Co** and palm-fringed **Canh Duong Beach**. This is one of the country's prettiest and most relaxing strands, and as yet it has not been overdeveloped.

Lang Co beach, near Danang

Just 18km (12 miles) from Lang Co, **Bach Ma National Park ❼** (www.bachma.vnn.vn; charge) has become one of Vietnam's best nature refuges, with 2,147 plant species, 894 insects, 358 birds, 132 mammals, 57 fish and more than 50 species of reptiles and amphibians identified thus far. It is best known, however, for the resident population of Edward's pheasants, once thought to have become extinct in the 1940s.

Beyond Lang Co the road climbs steeply to cross a spur of the Annamese Cordillera that juts into the South China Sea. This is the famous **Deo Hai Van** (Pass of the Clouds), so called because the 500m (1,625ft) high pass is often swathed in clouds and mist. In clear weather the views are remarkable. Until 1306, Hai Van formed the frontier between Vietnam and the Kingdom of Champa. It is also the geographic and climatic frontier between northern and southern Vietnam. To the north the winters are markedly colder and sometimes drier, while to the south winters tend to be warm and wet.

Unfortunately most buses now take the new tunnel and bypass Deo Hai Van.

Danang

Vietnam's fourth largest city and site of the country's third international airport, **Danang** ❽ (Da Nang) is a pleasant city with all the modern conveniences of Ho Chi Minh City but none of the crowds and far fewer hassles. Danang is surrounded by several natural areas that are also well worth exploring.

Bao Tang Dieu Khac Champa (Museum of Cham Sculpture; daily 8am–5pm; charge) is located on the western bank of Danang's Han River. Founded in 1915 by the Ecole Française d'Extrême Orient, this unique cultural treasure trove is currently in need of renovation, but remains a must-see destination for its unique collection of Cham statuary and bas-reliefs. Figures from the pantheon of Hindu deities, including Vishnu, Shiva, Uma, Ganesh and Nandi are a recurrent theme, as is the female breast, an important icon in Cham religious art. Perhaps most famous of all the carvings on display is the exquisite dancing *apsara* from the Cham capital, Tra Kieu, in the northwest corner of Gallery Three.

Son Tra Peninsula, known as Monkey Mountain to the US military, is a lush nature preserve northwest of Danang. The mountain is best explored by motorbike, with roads winding through dense rainforest and around steep cliffs. Macaques, civets, pheasants and cobras are among the many species easily seen here.

The entrance to a Marble Mountains shrine

The white sands of China Beach

The **Marble Mountains**, about 7km (4 miles) south of Danang, contain numerous caverns that have long housed a series of shrines dedicated to Buddha or to Confucius. Today the area is swamped with stone-carving factories, selling everything from one-tonne marble lions and Madonnas to stone chess sets and mortar and pestles.

China Beach, stretching 30km (18 miles) south of Danang, was once a favourite Rest and Recreation area for US servicemen during the Second Indochina War. Today it's under development with numerous new resorts and golf courses. It has some of the best surfing in the country, as well as great kiteboarding conditions.

Hoi An

Located on the Thu Bon River 30km (18 miles) south of Danang, **Hoi An ❾** was an important port under the Cham, more than 1000 years ago, and continued under the Nguyen kings. By the mid-19th century, however, the progressive silting up of the Thu Bon River and the development of nearby Danang combined to turn Hoi An into a backwater. The result is a delightful **old town** and a Unesco World Heritage Site. An inexpensive admission ticket gains you entry to all its old streets, one of the four museums, one of the four traditional houses, one of the assembly halls, the Handicraft Workshop and either the Japanese Covered Bridge or the Quan Cong Temple. Most sights are open 8am–5pm and closed for lunch between noon and 2pm.

Hoi An is renowned for its **traditional houses**. Best-known is **Nha Co Tan Ky** Ⓐ (Tan Ky House), a fine example of an 18th-century Sino-Viet shophouse built around a tiny central courtyard. It is distinguished by the elegant 'crab shell' ceiling and the exquisite mother-of-pearl inlay Chinese poetry hanging from the columns that support the roof. Nearby **Nha Co Phung Hung** Ⓑ (Phung Hung House) has been home to the same family for eight generations. Supported by 80 hardwood columns, this building shows Chinese influence in the gallery and shuttered windows; the delicate glass skylights are Japanese in style.

The Chinese merchants, who dominated the commerce of Hoi An, identified themselves with their native provinces, and built **assembly halls** to act as community centres and places of worship. Five distinct Overseas Chinese communities lived in Hoi An – Fujian, Guangdong, Hainan, Chaozhou and Hakka – and all except the latter had their

Street scene in Hoi An

Phuc Kien (Fujian) Assembly Hall

own assembly hall. **Hoi Quan Phuc Kien C** (Fujian Chinese Assembly Hall), founded in the late 17th century, is the most interesting. A large model of a wooden junk standing near the central altar serves to remind members of their cultural origins and how they first came to Hoi An.

Hoi An has a number of interesting museums. The **Bao Tang Van Hoa D** (Museum of Sa Huynh Culture) has a small collection of jewellery and pottery from excavations around Hoi An. The **Museum of Folklore E** is a large old house with a good craft shop on the lower floor, and an excellent museum upstairs. There are exhibits of ancient crafts, artisan tools and, of course, local folklore. **Bao Tang Gom Su** (Museum of Trading Ceramics) is located in a lovely traditional wooden house, with a modest display of broken ceramics and pottery shards.

Hoi An also has a number of small but interesting temples. These include **Chua Quan Cong F**, centrally located on Tran

Phu Street, which was established in 1653 and is dedicated to Quan Cong, a member of the Taoist pantheon who brings good luck and protects travellers.

Hoi An also retains a number of family chapels. These include the **Tran Family Chapel** on Le Loi Street which was established about two centuries ago as a shrine to venerate the ancestors of the Tran family who moved from China to Vietnam around 1700. The building shows clear signs of Chinese, Japanese and indigenous Vietnamese influence, as does the **Truong Family Chapel** on a nearby side street running south of Phan Chu Trinh Street.

The best-known historical monument in town is **Cau Nhat Ban** (Japanese Covered Bridge). Built in 1593 by Japanese merchants residing in Hoi An, this ochre-painted wooden bridge crosses a narrow side channel of the Thu Bon River. A small temple, **Chua Cau**, is incorporated in the northern side of the bridge.

One of Hoi An's most enticing features is its close proximity (5km/3 miles) to the lovely and only lightly developed **Cua Dai beach**. Rent a bicycle in town and pedal east out of town on Tran Hung Dao Street, which leads to Cua Dai Street. As you leave town, you will pass rice paddies and small villages straddling a beautiful estuary.

The Japanese Covered Bridge

The Central Coast

Vietnam's long central coast offers the visitor some of the country's finest beaches and a wide variety of fresh and delicious seafood. It is also rich in history. For over 1,000 years the whole

Ruins at My Son

of this beautiful region belonged to the Champa, a seafaring people who built a great Hindu civilisation to the east of the Annamese Cordillera. Over the centuries, as the Vietnamese pressed south, Champa was gradually conquered, forcing many of its citizens to take refuge in Ninh Thuan and Binh Thuan provinces, as well as nearby Cambodia, China and Malaysia. Had Champa kingdom survived, Indochina would still comprise four countries instead of three, but it was not to be. Today little remains of the lost kingdom other than the brick towers that dot the countryside and scattered communities of ethnic Cham, now a minority in a land they once ruled.

Cham temples follow one basic design. They represent Mt Meru, the Hindu Abode of the Gods, and face East towards the rising sun. The sanctum sanctorum, called *kalan* in Cham, normally had a Shiva *linga* at its centre. Temples usually had three storeys and were undecorated inside. The outer walls of brick and sandstone were carved with considerable skill.

About 40km (25 miles) southwest of Hoi An, beneath the curved peak of **Hon Quap** or Cat's Tooth Mountain, is **My Son ⑩**, site of the most significant surviving Cham monuments in Vietnam. My Son was an important religious centre between the 4th and 13th centuries, serving as a spiritual counterpart to the nearby Cham capital at **Tra Kieu**, of which little remains. Traces of around 70 temples and related structures may still be found at My Son, though only about 20 are still in relatively good condition – most of the others were severely damaged by American bombs during the Second Indochina War. My Son is fairly difficult to find, and although it's reached by metalled roads it is best to visit by taxi or minibus, arranged via tour operators in Hoi An or Danang, as the site is well off the beaten track. It's also rather exposed in spots, so in hot, sunny weather be sure to use sunscreen and wear a hat.

The most striking Cham monuments are the famed **Cham Towers**, tall sanctuaries made of bricks joined together in a mysterious fashion that still puzzles the experts, as no bonding material is visible. The best explanation offered to date is that the Cham master-builders used a form of resin to glue the bricks together. The coast of central Vietnam is studded with Cham Towers from My Son south to Phan Thiet.

Temple Statuary

Most Vietnamese temples contain several representations of Buddhas, distinguished by their elongated ear lobes, the presence of an *urna*, or third eye, in the middle of their foreheads, and their tightly curled hair. They are usually represented in one of the classical *mudras*, or attitudes, and seated on a throne, often in the lotus position.

Close by will be statues of the eight Kim Cang, or Genies of the Cardinal Directions, as well as various La Han, or Arhats, and Bo Tat, or Bodhisattvas. These are usually depicted as princes, wearing rich robes and crowns or headdresses. A popular image is Quan Cong, usually rosy-cheeked and green-cloaked, accompanied by his trusty companions, General Chau Xuong and the Mandarin Quan Binh, often with horse and groom.

Glittering roofs

At the height of Champa's glory, during the rule of Indravarman IV in the 12th century, the roofs of some of the temples at My Son were reportedly covered with a fine sheath of gold, no sign of which remains today.

For several years now, a long earth and stone rampart in the mountain foothills of **Quang Ngai Province** has been the focus of local and international researchers and archaeologists who have dated '**The Long Wall of Quang Ngai**' ⓫ (Vietnam's own 'Great Wall') as being approximately 200 years old, with forts along it dating even further back. The wall's largest sections measure 4m high and 6m wide. Its total length is 127km (79 miles).

Situated at the southern coastal tip of Binh Dinh Province, the capital city of **Quy Nhon** ⓬ (also spelled Qui Nhon) is an attractive fishing community on the way from Hoi An to Nha Trang with a plethora of ancient Cham temples. Right in the middle of a busy neighbourhood is an ancient Cham temple complex called **Thap Doi** (886 Tran Hung Dao; daily 8am–5pm; free). Built in the late 12th century, both towers have pyramidal peaks rather than the characteristic terracing found on most Cham towers.

The **Po Nagar Cham Temple** (daily 8am–6pm; charge) comprise one of the most important Cham sites in Vietnam, dating back to the 8th century. The temple is dedicated to the goddess Yang Ino Po Nagar and is still venerated by local people, both Viet and Cham.

The Po Nagar towers are about 2km (1.2 miles) north of **Nha Trang** ⓭, an attractive, medium-sized city of about 250,000 people with some of the best beaches in Vietnam. The city has a pleasant, laid-back feel to it and is increasingly populated with fine hotels and restaurants. Nha Trang is a great place to soak up the sun, enjoy the active nightlife and indulge in the freshest of seafood.

It's also one of the best spots in the country for water sports. The waters are relatively clear, and the offshore islands are ideal for snorkelling, scuba diving and fishing. It's easy to hire boats and there are more than 70 islands to explore. The nearest of them, and the most easily accessible by ferry, is **Hon Mieu**. The main attraction here is the **Tri Nguyen Aquarium** (charge), a pond blocked off from the sea by a dam and divided into three separate sections filled with starfish, turtles, sharks and other marine life. Slightly further out to sea, **Hon Mun** is popular with locals and visitors alike and offers such activities as parasailing, waterskiing, snorkelling, jet-skiing and, of course, sunbathing. The largest island in the small archipelago, **Hon Tre**, is the site of the **Vinpearl Resort Nha Trang**. The island is reached by a 3,320m (10,892ft) gondola ride, which holds the world record for the longest ocean-crossing cable car. The resort's **Vinpearl Land Amusement Park** (daily

Watersports on Nha Trang's main beach

Po Ro Me Cham Tower

8am–10pm; charge; www.vinpearlland.com) contains carnival rides, a roller coaster, waterpark, outdoor shopping centre and several restaurants. The central feature is the **Underwater World Aquarium** (separate charge) with more than 20 freshwater and marine tanks, including an impressive walk-through tank featuring rays, sharks, moray eels and a large variety of reef fish.

Still further south, beyond Cam Ranh Bay – one of the finest natural harbours in Southeast Asia and, in Cold War times, a scene of rivalry between the US and Soviet navies – the twin towns of **Phan Rang** ⑭ and **Thap Cham** form the modern homeland of the Cham people, and are also known chiefly for the excellence of the local grapes. About 7km (4 miles) out of town a well-preserved and highly-venerated Cham monument stands at **Po Klong Garai**. About 15km (10 miles) south of Phan Rang is another important tower at **Po Ro Me**.

The last significant Cham monument in southern Vietnam may be found at the 8th-century **Thap Poshanu Cham Temple** overlooking **Phan Thiet**, 146km (91 miles) south of Phan Rang. This quiet coastal city has a large and colourful fishing fleet, best viewed from Tran Hung Dao Bridge in the city centre. The town is also famous for its odorous *nuoc mam* fish sauce and dragon fruit cactus plantations. Phan Thiet is a centre for the ancient whale-worshipping religion of Vietnamese fisherman. Van Thuy Tu, located near the city port, is one of the largest whale temples in the country, with a whale skeleton reconstructed and on display. The biennial Cau Ngu festival is held at the temple, usually in May.

Of greater significance to most visitors, Phan Thiet is also the gateway to **Mui Ne** ⓯ (www.muinebeach.net), one of the finest beaches in Vietnam and the country's premier holiday resort area. A curving white beach stretches for 12km (7.5 miles) to the cape at Mui Ne fishing village, and has become the base for the kite-boarding and watersports capital of Vietnam. North of Mui Ne is a vast sea of red, white and golden sand dunes that make for magical photographs at dusk and dawn.

The picturesque **Khe Ga** lighthouse, located 45 minutes south of the Phan Thiet on a rocky islet, is the tallest in Vietnam (built by the French in 1897). **Ta Cu Mountain**, equally distant and to the east, hides a grand pagoda and the country's largest reclining Buddha, reachable by gondola.

Writing Vietnamese

The influence of Vietnam's northern neighbour meant that the Vietnamese language was once written in Chinese characters known as *chu nho*. All manuscripts and government documents used *chu nho* – even after independence in the 10th century. In the 13th century the poet Nguyen Thuyen developed a distinct though complex Vietnamese script called *chu nom*, based on Chinese characters.

A radical change came in the mid-17th century when Alexandre de Rhodes, a French Jesuit missionary, developed a Roman script known as quoc ngu. Initially it was used only by the Catholic Church and, after about 1860, the colonial administration. The study of quoc ngu became compulsory in secondary schools in 1906, and two years later the royal court in Hue ordered a new curriculum, written entirely in quoc ngu. It became the national written language in 1919 and is used throughout the country today.

Dalat and Around

Dalat ⑯ (Da Lat) is Vietnam's premier mountain resort. Set by the banks of the Cam Ly River at an altitude of 1,500m (4,875ft), it makes a refreshing change from the heat and humidity of the Central Coast and Ho Chi Minh City. The hill station was first established at the beginning of the 20th century. It was popular with the French, and remains even more so with the Vietnamese.

It's very pleasant to take a stroll around central Dalat. The town retains a Gallic flavour, particularly in the former **French Quarter** around Phan Dinh Phung. The **Dalat Cathedral** on Tran Phu Road is also reminiscent of the colonial era. Completed in 1942, it is dedicated to St Nicolas and has a 47m (153ft) high spire and stained glass windows.

Dalat's **Central Market** (Cho Da Lat; daily 6am–10pm) is one of the largest in the country, set in a deep hollow of a hillside and surrounded by rows of cafés and shops selling wine and candied fruit. The second floor of the middle building is devoted entirely to food stalls. The ground floor of the market sells fresh produce grown in the surrounding region: strawberries, tomatoes, avocados, asparagus and just about any fruit, flower and vegetable found in countries with temperate climates.

Across town, the **Lam Dong Museum** (daily 7.30–11.30am, 1.30–4.30pm; charge) has been recognised by the United Nations for its extensive collections of musical gongs used by the local K'ho, Ma and Churu minorities. Other exhibits include an impressive taxidermy collection of local wildlife; ancient relics from the Funan (or Champa) empire excavated near Cat Tien National Park; Champa artefacts found in recent excavations from throughout the province; and full-sized Ma and K'ho tribal longhouses.

Nga's Crazy House (daily 7am–6pm; charge), with its whimsical architecture, is continuously being added to, with tunnels, stairways and halls meandering into secret rooms and towers, and reading nooks occupied by statues of giant kangaroos, giraffes, eagles and bears.

Nearby, the **Dalat Cable Car** (Cap Treo Dalat; Tue–Fri 7.30–11.30am, 1.30–5pm, Mon 7.30–11.30am; charge), stretches for 2.3km (1.5 miles), providing expansive views of mountain forests and garden villages, all the way to **Thien Vien Truc Lam** (Bamboo Forest Meditation Centre). The Zen monastery was built in 1993 and houses nearly 80 nuns and 100 monks. Below the monastery is a picnic area with chairs and tables, overlooking the tranquil **Paradise Lake**. The cable car is located less than 3km (2 miles) south of the town centre.

Hang Nga Crazy House, Dalat

Dalat was the favoured holiday retreat of Bao Dai, the last of the Nguyen Emperors (1926–45), who enjoyed hunting in the surrounding hills. He ordered the construction of a large villa set amidst pine trees about 2km (1.2 miles) out of town. Completed in 1933, the villa, generally known as **Bao Dai's Summer Palace** (daily 7.30–11am, 1.30–4pm; charge), is open to the public. The former imperial living quarters are on the first floor, and here the visitor can see busts of Bao Dai and his uncle Khai Dinh, together with assorted family pictures.

About 12km (7 miles) northwest of Dalat, at the foot of Lang Bian Mountain, are a group of small settlements which

Elephant Falls, outside Dalat, in full flow

make up **Lat Village**. The village is inhabited by people of the K'ho Lat minority, as well as by members of related minority groups, the Ma and the Chill. The villagers, who make a living by growing rice, coffee, beans and yams, are known for their pottery and iron-working skills.

The most easily visited minority settlement is **Lang Ga**, conveniently located just off the highway from Dalat to the coast. It is also known as **Chicken Village**, after the large statue of a cockerel that dominates the surrounding houses. The local K'ho people are skilled weavers and sell a variety of woven and embroidered goods.

The hills surrounding Dalat are blessed by an abundance of beautiful waterfalls. **Tiger Falls** (Thac Hang Cop), is 14km (9 miles) from town, and is both the grandest and the least visited of all the local waterfalls. **Datanla Waterfall** is just a few hundred metres past the turn-off for Thien Vien Truc Lam. Overlook the pony rides, men in cheap bear suits and girls in fake minority costumes, and instead enjoy the toboggan run to the falls and back. **Elephant Falls** (Thac Vo) is 30km (19 miles) west of Dalat. A shop above the falls sells beautiful hand-woven K'ho blankets and crafts with elephant motifs, all made on-site.

HO CHI MINH CITY

After national consolidation in 1975, the Communist authorities extended the municipal boundaries of the former Saigon so that **Ho Chi Minh City**  is now a small province extending from the South China Sea almost to the Cambodian frontier. In practice, however, most southerners continue to refer to downtown Ho Chi Minh City as 'Saigon', while the traditional Chinatown area further to the west remains familiarly known as 'Cholon'.

Just as the north is dominated by Hanoi, so Ho Chi Minh City dominates the south. Yet here the similarity ends. Where Hanoi is ancient, Ho Chi Minh City is relatively modern. While Hanoi has traditionally been conservative, Ho Chi Minh City is much more willing to embrace new trends and fashions. It is a great city for wining, dining and shopping, but there's much less of historical and cultural interest than in Hanoi.

Ho Chi Minh City is Vietnam's economic powerhouse

Downtown Saigon

Central Saigon was almost as much a creation of France as of Vietnam, but the city's rather distinguished colonial style acquired something of an American flavour between 1954 and 1975 when Saigon served as the capital of the US-backed Republic of Vietnam. The Saigonese are a lively people, more intent on doing business and improving their standard of living than on worrying about the past. A good place to start an exploration of the downtown area is the **Song Saigon** or

A statue of Ho Chi Minh in the city that now bears his name

Saigon River. Here one can watch the hustle and bustle of life on the waterfront as small craft jostle for space with larger ocean-going ships and hydrofoils bound for the nearby resort of Vung Tau.

Running about a kilometre from Le Duan Street to the Saigon River through the heart of District 1 and original French Quarter, **Dong Khoi Street** (Duong Dong Khoi) is the city's main commercial drag. This wide, tree-lined boulevard is lined with historical sights, shops, galleries, cafés and luxury hotels. During French colonial times, this was known as the elegant Rue Catinat, the epicentre of colonial life and where the French built some of their most important buildings.

Dong Khoi leads directly to **Nha Tho Duc Ba Ⓐ** (Notre Dame Cathedral, daily 8–11am, 2–5pm; free), built by the French in 1883. Check out the splendid **General Post Office Ⓑ** (Buu Dien Saigon, daily 7am–10pm) just east of the cathedral; **Nha Hat Thanh Pho Ⓒ** (Municipal Theatre) on Lam Son Square between three of Saigon's most distinguished hotels, the **Continental, Rex Ⓓ** and the **Caravelle**; and the magnificent **Uy Ban Nhan Dan Thanh Pho Ho Chi Minh** (Ho Chi Minh People's Committee) Ⓔ at the northern end of Nguyen Hue Boulevard.

In the centre of town stands **Dinh Thong Nhat** ➐ (Reunification Palace; daily 7.30–11am, 1–4pm; charge), once the official residence of the former Presidents of South Vietnam. Guided tours in English and French will take you from underground war-planning and communications rooms to cavernous banquet rooms and reception halls, to grand sitting and dining rooms, libraries and a theatre. In the grounds stand two T54 tanks of the kind that broke into the former palace in April 1975.

Two blocks north of the Reunification Palace at 28 Vo Van Tan Street is **Bao Tang Chung Tich Chien Tranh** ➒ (War Remnants Museum; daily 7.30am–noon and 1.30–5pm; charge). A visit here is a sobering reminder of the heavy toll of war. This was hurriedly opened as the Museum of American War Crimes after reunification in 1975. Its controversial name was changed in 1997 as part of conditions dictated by the US government over trade pacts. Exhibit halls display the

Saigon, the Southern Capital

Three hundred years ago Saigon was no more than a small Khmer fishing settlement called Prey Nokor, a name still widely applied by Cambodian nationalists to the city today. When a group of Chinese refugees from the Qing Empire arrived in the region, the Cambodian governor turned for advice and help to the Nguyen Lords of Hue. The price of settling the Chinese and restoring order was Vietnamese suzerainty. Later the city expanded to join with the nearby Chinese settlement of Cholon – Saigon has always had a strong Chinese flavour to it.

In 1859 the city was seized by France and soon became the capital of the French colony of Cochinchina. Briefly, between 1956 and 1975, Saigon functioned as the capital of the anti-communist Republic of Vietnam. Since the communist seizure of power in 1975, however, it is has once again become overshadowed by its long-term rival Hanoi.

Buddhist Xa Loi Pagoda

horrors of both the French and American wars; including graphic photographs, bell jars of deformed foetuses showing the effects of US-sprayed chemical defoliants, plus a guillotine used by the French and mock-up of the notorious 'tiger cages'.

Downtown Saigon isn't noted for its temples, but northwest of the colonial heart of the city, along the broad boulevard named Dien Bien Phu, there are two that are worth visiting. **Chua Ngoc Huang**  (Pagoda of the Jade Emperor), is on Mai Thi Luu off the northern end of Dien Bien Phu near Rach Thi Cawal – and, incidentally, by the Dakao Bridge where Graham Greene's fictional Quiet American, Alden Pyle, was found murdered. Built in 1909, this spectacularly colourful Chinese temple is dedicated to Ngoc Huang, the Jade Emperor of the Taoist pantheon. Near the southern end of Dien Bien Phu on Huyen Thanh Quan is **Xa Loi Pagoda**, a Vietnamese temple with murals depicting scenes from the life of the Buddha.

Right in the centre of Downtown Saigon, **Ben Thanh Market** ❶ epitomises the irrepressibly capitalist nature of Ho Chi Minh City. The largest covered market in town, it is packed to overflowing with stalls selling all manner of wares to hundreds of shoppers. Some locals still shop here, but now there are mostly souvenirs for sale – conical *non la* hats, silk *ao dai* costumes, silk-screened T-shirts, coffee from Dalat and a range of imitation antiquities.

To the northeast, **Bao Tang Lich Su** ❿ (Museum of Vietnamese History; Tue–Sun 8–11.30am, 1.30–4.30pm;

charge) on Nguyen Binh Kiem houses an impressive collection of artefacts from the Bronze-Age Dong Son culture through the intervening Oc Eo culture to the coming of the Chams, the Khmers and finally the Vietnamese. The exhibits here include a collection of Buddha images from various Asian countries. Art lovers should head for the **Bao Tang My Thuat** Ⓚ (Fine Arts Museum; Tue–Sun 9am–4.30pm; charge) on Pho Duc Chinh. Housed in an attractive but somewhat dilapidated yellow-and-white colonial building, its exhibits include contemporary Vietnamese art, abstract art, Socialist Realism and historic artefacts from Oc Eo, Cambodia and Champa.

Cholon

About 6km (4 miles) west of downtown Saigon lies the bustling quarter of **Cholon**, Ho Chi Minh City's Chinatown. From the end of the 18th century Overseas Chinese from the

Daily life in Cholon

coastal provinces of southern China settled in this region, establishing a township physically and ethnically distinct from nearby Saigon. The two have long since merged into a single metropolis, but Cholon retains a distinctly Chinese flavour, especially in and around its temples.

Set in the heart of Cholon, **Chua Ong Nghia An** ⬤ serves the local Chaozhou community and is chiefly notable for its gilded woodwork. Its shady interior is dominated by huge hanging spirals of incense which burn for up to a month. Just across the road the 19th-century **Hoi Quan Tam Son Temple** ⬤ serves the local Fujian community and is dedicated to Me Sanh, the Goddess of Fertility. Local women come to this faded but richly ornamented temple to pray for children. A short distance to the northwest stands **Thien Hau Pagoda**, built in the early 19th century to serve Cholon's substantial Cantonese community.

Binh Tay Market ⬤ at 57A Thap Muoi Street is Cholon's biggest market and best epitomises its vibrant commercialism. Built in 1928, its exterior is a fine example of early 20th-century Chinese-influenced French architecture: oriental-style multi-tiered roofs stalked by serpentine dragons blend with distinctive French mustard-yellow walls and a clock tower with four clock faces.

North of Cholon by the southern shore of Dam Sen Lake, **Giac Vien Pagoda** ⬤ is one of the oldest temples in Ho Chi Minh City, founded about two centuries ago. Nguyen Emperor Gia Long is said to have worshipped here. Still further north, in the bleak suburb of Tan Binh, **Giac Lam Pagoda** ⬤ dates from 1744 and is said to be the oldest temple in the entire Saigon-Cholon region.

DAY TRIPS FROM HO CHI MINH CITY

There are four interesting excursions in the vicinity of Ho Chi Minh City. To the east the seaside resort town of Vung

Tau offers sun, swimming and seafood. A short flight to the Con Dao Islands takes you to an infamous prison now turned into a marine reserve. To the northwest, the claustrophobic tunnels of Cu Chi are a sobering reminder of the Indochina Wars. A short distance further northwest, Tay Ninh is home to the extraordinary Holy See of the Cao Dai religion.

Southeast of Ho Chi Minh City

The resort town of **Vung Tau**  lies at the tip of a triangular peninsula jutting into the sea near the mouth of the Saigon River. Hydrofoils leave from the junction of the Saigon River and the Kinh Ben Creek in central Saigon on a regular basis. The journey takes around 90 minutes and provides a good opportunity to catch glimpses of everyday life in the small riverine fishing villages en route.

Tranquillity reigns in the Con Dao Archipelago

Part of the Cu Chi tunnel network is open to visitors

Vung Tau or Boat Bay owes its development as a resort to the proximity of Ho Chi Minh City. Also partly industrialised, it is home to a major offshore oil company and a large fishing fleet. The beaches are not too bad, but at the same time they are unexceptional by Vietnamese standards. The fresh seafood, on the other hand, is excellent. Like Phan Thiet, Vung Tau has a famous temple devoted to whale worship. **Dinh Than Thang-Tam** (daily 8am–5pm; free) was built during the Minh Mang Dynasty (1820–1840) and is decorated with beautiful murals of dragons and sea monsters. A small whale skeleton is prominently on display in a glass case.

The **Con Dao Archipelago** ⑲ is made up of 16 islands around 100km (60 miles) off the coast of Vietnam. Once an infamous French prison known as 'Devil's Island', the wards were kept in inhumane conditions, including underground boxes known as 'tiger cages'. Today the island is a pristine resort getaway, and not yet flooded with tourists due to the limited availability of flights from Saigon, though celebrity visits from the likes of Brad Pitt and Angelina Jolie are helping to put it on the map. WWF has a programme here to protect sea turtles, although a significant number of them still end up in restaurants and souvenir shops.

Northwest of Ho Chi Minh City

About 35km (22 miles) west of Ho Chi Minh City, the district of **Cu Chi** ⑳ is famous for its extensive underground tunnel network. During the Second Indochina War, the National Liberation Front managed to dig a complex network of underground passages, dormitories, kitchens, munitions factories and hospitals close to Saigon, in spite of constant attacks by South Vietnamese and US forces. The tunnel network has been claimed to have been vast, comprising more than 200km (124 miles) of narrow passageways stretching from the fringes of Ho Chi Minh City to the Cambodian border.

Today two sections of the Cu Chi tunnel network have been renovated and opened to visitors, one at **Ben Dinh** and the

Black Teeth, White Teeth

Chewing areca nut is an increasingly rare custom in Vietnam. Yet not so long ago, areca nut taken with the leaf of the betel tree and lime paste was consumed throughout the country. Chinese sources from the 6th century describe Vietnam as a region of betel-users, noting that the Chams 'constantly chewed betel', and during the same period Vietnamese fighters, engaged in yet another war with the Chinese, sang a martial song which emphasised this separate identity in the clearest of terms: *Fight to keep our hair long, Fight to keep our teeth black!*

The gradual demise of betel may be traced to the arrival of tobacco, which was first brought to the region in the mid-16th century. Vietnamese men took to tobacco with enthusiasm and betel chewing became increasingly associated with women. Thus, in the mid-19th century ladies of the Vietnamese court at Hue sported their blackened teeth with pride. The emperor informed a priest unwise enough remark on this that 'even a dog can have white teeth'. In Vietnam white teeth, now so highly prized, were once associated with dogs, ghosts – and Europeans.

other at nearby **Ben Duoc**. A Vietnamese in NLF uniform will guide you to an area of brush or low trees and ask you to locate an entrance to the tunnels. This is far from easy, and few Westerners could pass through the entrance even if they found it. But the enterprising Vietnamese, both proud of their military success at Cu Chi and keen to attract tourists, have enlarged several sections of tunnel to accommodate larger Westerners. The tunnels are still claustrophobic, humid and bat-filled, however, so few visitors will want to stay long underground.

Tay Ninh ㉑, about 50km (31 miles) beyond Cu Chi and 96km (60 miles) from central Ho Chi Minh City, is the headquarters of Vietnam's most idiosyncratic religion. Founded in 1926 by a Vietnamese mystic named Ngo Minh Chieu, Cao Dai is a uniquely Vietnamese philosophy. Cao Dai draws upon traditional Sino-Vietnamese Confucianism for its moral precepts and Taoism for its occult practices. Buddhism supplies the doctrines of karma and rebirth. The hierarchical organisation of the church, which includes a pope as supreme patriarch, archbishops and cardinals, is adopted from Roman Catholicism. Cao Dai's amazing number of saints include Buddha, Confucius, Jesus, Pericles, Julius Caesar, Joan of Arc, Napoleon Bonaparte, William Shakespeare, Victor Hugo and Sun Yat-sen. The supreme deity is represented as an all-seeing eye in a triangle.

Within a year of its founding Cao Dai had more than 25,000 followers, and by the 1950s almost 15 percent of all South Vietnamese were followers. By the end of the First Indochina War in 1954, Tay Ninh Province had become an almost independent Cao Dai fiefdom, where the sect's leadership controlled a private army 25,000 strong. The Cao Dai remained generally aloof from the struggle in the Second Indochina War, and as a consequence suffered considerable persecution following the communist seizure of power. It is estimated that there are 2.5 to 3 million followers of Cao Dai in Vietnam, worshipping at more than 400 temples.

Than That Cao Dai or the Great Cao Dai Temple, also commonly referred to as the Holy See, stands 4km (2.5 miles) east of the Tay Ninh city centre. Prayers are conducted four times daily at 6am, noon, 6pm and midnight, but visitors should try to attend the noon session as the Cao Dai authorities prefer this and also permit photography. The temple, which rises in nine levels, is richly, some might say gaudily, decorated. Certainly it is surreal, an elaborate pastiche of divine eyes, Cao Dai saints, dragon-swathed pillars and vaulted ceilings.

THE MEKONG DELTA

Broad, fertile and criss-crossed by a thousand waterways, the great delta of the Mekong River forms the southernmost

Worshippers at the Great Cao Dai Temple, Tay Ninh

part of Vietnam extending to Mui Ca Mau, the cape where the waters of the South China Sea meet those of the Gulf of Thailand. The vast delta region is made up of rich alluvial silt carried down by the floodwaters of the Mekong from neighbouring Cambodia, Laos and Thailand, Burma and China. So regular is this process that the delta is growing at a rate of about 75m (245ft) per year, extending both the shoreline and the rich farmlands of 'Vietnam's Rice Bowl'. A visit to this region enables the traveller to explore shaded waterways and floating markets by boat, see relics of the ancient Funanese city of Oc Eo, and visit Khmer Buddhist temples, Cham Muslim mosques and Hoa Hao temples.

The town of **My Tho** ㉒ is a sprawling market town by the banks of Cua Tien River just 60km (38 miles) southwest of Ho Chi Minh City. After hectic Saigon, My Tho is relatively quiet and a convenient place to explore local waterways and islands. There's not a lot to see in My Tho, although the huge and bustling market provides an interesting insight into delta lifestyles. My Tho's elaborate **Cao Dai Temple** is certainly worth visiting, similarly the pastel-coloured, colonial-period Catholic church and the immaculately maintained **Vinh Trang** Buddhist Pagoda.

The city of **Vinh Long** ㉓ is about 60km (38 miles) southwest of My Tho, accessible via an impressive suspension bridge across the broad Tien Giang, or Upper Mekong River. This is a reasonable overnight stop as there are several adequate hotels and a couple of good restaurants. Vinh Long is famous for the picturesque **Cai Be floating market** about an hour by boat from the city docks. The market functions from around 5am to 5pm, but it's best to visit in the early morning.

Mekong base camp

Can Tho makes a good place from which to explore. Accommodation available is the best in the delta and there are several good restaurants.

Waterside residences in My Tho

Another worthwhile boat trip is to nearby **Anh Binh Island**. Easily reached by small boats waiting on the shore, the island is very fertile and supports many vegetable gardens and fruit orchards. Boat trips to Cai Be usually stop off at a number of small factories manufacturing local specialities such as spring roll wrappers, rice popcorn, and coconut-based sweets. About 2km (1.2 miles) south of town by the banks of the Rach Long Canal stands **Van Thanh Mieu**, a rather run-down temple dedicated – unusually for the south – to Confucius.

Can Tho ㉔, 34km (21 miles) southwest of Vinh Long, is the largest town and *de facto* capital of the Mekong Delta. There's a domestic airport set amidst the myriad waterways, and boat or ferry connections can be made to almost anywhere in the delta. Here, too, the presence of Vietnam's substantial Khmer minority is apparent. **Munirangsyaram Pagoda** on Hoa Binh Street is the centre of Theravada Buddhism in the city, which

Travel by boat to experience the Mekong Delta

has an ethnic Khmer population of around 2,500. There are two interesting floating markets within easy striking distance of Can Tho. These are **Cai Rang**, about 5km (3 miles) southeast of the city, and **Phong Dien**, the most traditional floating market in the delta, situated about 20km (12 miles) southwest of the city.

About 60km (38 miles) northwest of Can Tho, the town of **Long Xuyen** 🕮 has little to offer, but is a necessary transit point on the way northwest to the Cambodian Frontier. Nearby are the ruins of **Oc Eo**, an important trading port of the Kingdom of Funan which dominated much of the Gulf of Siam coast and the Mekong Delta between the 2nd and 6th centuries. Today little remains of this once great settlement – the passage of time and shifting waters of the Mekong have obliterated all but pottery shards and some pilings. What survives of Funan culture is better viewed at the Museum of Vietnamese History in Ho

Chi Minh City and the National Museum of Vietnamese History in Hanoi.

Chau Doc ❷⓺ is another delta town, located on the banks of the Hau Giang or Lower Mekong close by the Cambodian frontier. Until the mid-18th century Chau Doc, like much of the Mekong Delta, was under Cambodian suzerainty. There's still a definite of border atmosphere about the place, and an interesting racial mix. The town is predominantly Vietnamese, but is also home to sizeable Hoa (Chinese), Cham and especially Khmer minorities.

The religious mix is still more eclectic. There are Vietnamese and Chinese Mahayana Buddhists, Cambodian Theravada Buddhists, Chinese and Vietnamese Catholics, Cham Muslims, Vietnamese and Khmer Cao Dai and – strangest of all – Hoa Hao, followers of the second major religious sect indigenous to the Mekong Delta. The Hoa Hao derive their designation from the small village of **Hoa Hao** some 20km (12 miles) east of Chau Doc. Hoa Hao advocates a return to the Theravada ideal of personal salvation combined with aspects of Confucianism and Ancestor Worship.

Boat Tours in the Mekong Delta

The highlights of boat trips around the Mekong are visiting the many fruit orchards and floating markets (as well as the ethnic Khmer Krom and Cham Bani communities). In floating markets, merchants (mostly women) sit in long wooden sampans and sell all manner of goods that you might find at any terrestrial market, including fish and meats, fruit and vegetables, clothing and household wares.

Most visitors (including independent backpackers) end up seeing the Mekong as part of an organised tour; either three days or five. The experience suggested here should take about three days.

WHAT TO DO

Vietnam is well on the way to becoming a shopper's paradise. In 1975, the victory of the communist north ushered in an era of austerity and deprivation. Private enterprise was banned and imported goods became an unattainable luxury. Not surprisingly, the economy fell to previously uncharted depths. The situation started to improve following the introduction of *doi moi* economic reforms in 1986. Early visitors to the new Vietnam were pestered by street hawkers and swarms of unfortunate children with little more to offer than postcards and stamps. Fortunately for both Vietnamese merchants and foreign visitors, all this has changed.

SHOPPING

Markets and Malls

Prices are generally reasonable in Vietnam. Traditionally, you would be expected to haggle, and this is still the case in markets and backstreet antiques shops – but don't expect huge discounts, as the naturally astute Vietnamese are stubborn salespeople and a two-price system generally exists for foreigners and resident Vietnamese. By contrast, haggling is not expected – or accepted – in obviously fixed-price places such as the new, air-conditioned shopping malls that populate downtown Hanoi and Saigon, and this is the case in smaller cities, too.

Vietnamese shop for groceries early in the morning. Market shopping tends to be more relaxed in the afternoons when the traders have cooled off a little. In the cities, shopping hours are usually 7.30–11.30am and 1.30–6pm, but increasingly shops and malls stay open until 8pm or later.

The upmarket Ipa Nima boutique in Hanoi

Dalat's central food market

Travellers cheques and credit cards are increasingly accepted in Vietnam, although primarily in large cities and at larger hotels and restaurants. While US dollars are generally accepted anywhere, using Vietnamese dong will ensure you get more value for your money.

What to Buy

Traditional Vietnamese handicrafts offer a wide variety of wares to choose from. These include paintings (lacquer, oil, gouache and silk), mother-of-pearl, ceramics, pottery, carved wood, embroidery, bamboo and wickerwork, baskets, sculpture, jewellery, jade (often fake), silks and brocades. You might like to consider adding a *non la*, the ubiquitous Vietnamese conical hat, or an *ao dai*, the traditional costume worn by Vietnamese women, to your wardrobe.

Fake war souvenirs are common – especially Zippo lighters and US army dog tags. Enduringly popular and very reasonably priced, T-shirts featuring Vietnamese flags and Socialist Realist designs are available just about everywhere. Clothing is comparatively cheap and local tailors can very quickly produce well-made garments to the design of your choice.

Antiquities are sold but often those found in shops are fakes. They are also heavily regulated and should not be purchased without receipts. Antiques shops in the centre of Ho Chi Minh City and the old quarter of Hanoi sell Vietnamese wood or Laotian bronze Buddhas, old porcelain, ivory carvings, items of silver, small jade statuettes and objects used by the various cults. Increasingly these 'antiques' are clever copies of the real thing, which is good for Vietnam and should satisfy most visitors. Bear in mind that it is forbidden to export certain objects and in principle clearance must be obtained before taking antiquities out of the country.

An unusual and attractive souvenir manufactured mostly in the south and available at Ben Thanh Market is a bamboo screen designed to hang across doorways. Made of hundreds of tiny bamboo cylinders strung on long threads, they are painstakingly painted to show a typical Vietnamese theme – girls dressed in *non la* hats and *ao dai*, for example, or a blossom tree. Considering the work involved, they are very reasonably priced.

Where to Shop

Hanoi. The Old Quarter – bordered by the railway line and the north side of Hoan Kiem Lake – is filled with little boutiques and stalls overflowing with an astonishing array of goods. Cheap Chinese electronic products, food, baskets, clothes, Chinese herbal medicines,

Top-class tipples

Russian vodkas and top-quality French wines and champagne are available at very reasonable prices. Vietnamese coffee is cheap, delicious and makes an excellent souvenir.

Bat Trang pottery village, one of several specialist craft villages outside Hanoi

even marble tombstones. Dong Xuan Market, Hanoi's main covered market, was recently rebuilt after being damaged by fire, and is once again open for business.

Buy silk from shops in Hang Gai Street. Hang Quat Street has red candlesticks and brightly-coloured funeral banners for temple use. Hang Dao stationers have pressed ink blocks, some decorated with gold leaf. You can also find good Chinese paintbrushes for calligraphy or painting. Further south Trang Tien Street is a good area to explore, with some of the best ceramics in town. Red split bamboo plates and bowls make unusual gifts. Down the alleys you will find photocopied and original books and maps, some antique. T-shirts feature political images, such as Ho Chi Minh or Vietnam's national flag (a gold star on a red background).

Vietnam certainly has more art galleries than any other Southeast Asian country. Hanoi is the main centre for this activity, though Ho Chi Minh City and Hoi An are also note-worthy centres for the Fine Arts. Styles vary from traditional Vietnamese painting through Impressionism and Modern Art to Socialist Realism. Galleries in Hanoi can be found around Hoan Kiem Lake, especially to the south and west of the lake.

Hue. Look for the unique 'poem hats' which make an excel-lent and inexpensive souvenir. In Hue the characteristic *non la* conical hats worn by Vietnamese women everywhere are par-ticularly fine and some may be held up to the light to reveal traditional scenes or poems in silhouette. Also noteworthy are the rice paper and silk paintings. It's best to look for antiques, pseudo-antiques and clothing in the newer part of town, south of the Perfume River. For colourful and traditional markets, head north of the river to the Old City.

Danang and Hoi An. In Danang reasonably priced replicas of Cham statues are available at the Cham Museum souvenir shop. Hoi An is famous for its cotton cloth and silk boutiques and tailors. If you're looking for tailor-made clothing this is an excel-lent place to come. Hoi An has numerous art galleries, although for more serious art and well-known artists, try Hanoi and Ho Chi Minh City. Hoi An's entire old town has become a shop-per's paradise where you can find every sort of souvenir available in Vietnam.

Nha Trang. Local delicacies and traditional wares are available at the Dam Market. Jewellery and decorations made from shells are found along the esplanade and at Cau Da Port. 'Tortoise-shell' necklaces really are made from turtle shell, despite

Non la, the ubiquitous Vietnamese conical hat

Marble figurines are made on Marble Mountain near Danang

regulations to stop this. By contrast, the ivory-like material used in jewellery is actually fish bone. As elsewhere in Vietnam, there are 24-hour tailor shops and T-shirts for sale, but Nha Trang is a beach resort with few pretensions as a cultural centre.

Dalat. The Central Market in Dalat has a plethora of wares, from candied fruit and local wines to deer jerky and souvenirs. The three-storey structure (food on the middle floor, souvenirs and clothes above and below) dates from 1958 and is found at the junction of Nguyen Thi Minh Khai and Le Dai Hanh. Dalat is famous for its roses and other flowers, sold around the outside of the ground floor.

Strawberries are abundant – candied, as syrup, turned to wine or blended in fresh strawberry milkshakes. Artichokes are grown here and made into tea called *tra atiso* or *actiso*. You may also want to try the locally-produced Vang Dalat, or Dalat wine. XQ Historical Village (tel: 063-383 1343; www.xqhandembroidery.com) is a must-visit for silk embroidery.

Ho Chi Minh City. This city is a great destination for shoppers. Almost everything, from computer hardware and software, through cameras, imported clothes and pseudo war paraphernalia may be found in the city centre or in Cholon. Dong Khoi and the streets immediately off it have the best

souvenir shops. You will find silks, lacquerware and embroi-
deries in abundance. The best place for inexpensive clothing is
the huge Ben Thanh Market. Tailors all over the city are good
and many speak English, so take the opportunity to have some
clothes made for a fraction the cost you would pay at home –
allow 24–48 hours for an order to be filled. Popular shopping
malls include Vincom Shopping Centre on Dong Khoi Street,
Hung Vuong Plaza near Cholon and The Paragon in District 7.

Antiques and especially pseudo-antiques abound. Best to
head for Le Cong Kieu near Ben Thanh Market for lower
prices and a less frenetic atmosphere.

ENTERTAINMENT

Performing Arts

Vietnam has relatively few performance centres with regular
schedules. Most of Vietnam's cultural entertainment is performed for local television or festivals in the lunar calendar.

Vietnam is most famous
for water puppetry, or *mua
roi nuoc*, best seen in Hanoi at
the Thang Long Water Puppet
Theatre (57b Dinh Tien
Hoang; www.thanglongwater-
puppet.org), although smaller
shows are available in Hue
at the Century Hotel (49 Le
Loi). Royal court music, or *ca
Hue*, can be seen in Hue at the
Royal Theater in the Citadel,
and nightly at the Hotel
Saigon Morin (30 Le Loi) or
Tropical Garden Restaurant
(27 Chu Van An). Traditional

A White Tai dance performance
at Mai Chau in northwest Vietnam

Hanoi's Funky Buddha bar

song and dance shows are also popular in Hoi An during the day at the Artcraft Manufacturing Workshop (9 Nguyen Thai Hoc) and nightly at the Traditional Arts Theatre (75 Nguyen Thai Hoc).

Nightlife

Until 1990 Vietnam had very little nightlife worth speaking of, but since then things have started to change. Before 1975 Saigon was a pretty wild place, with bars, nightclubs and girls on every street corner. All this was swept away by the communist victory, but 15 years of Stalinist orthodoxy didn't change the Saigonese very much, and nowadays Ho Chi Minh City and Hanoi has nightclubs, discos and karaoke bars aplenty.

Hanoi was always a more staid city than its southern sister, but today the capital is lightening up, though at a slower pace. Nightlife in Hanoi revolves around wining and dining at the many new restaurants, bars and clubs, particularly in and around the old quarter and neighbourhoods encircling Hoan Kiem Lake and West Lake.

At weekends, youth culture in Ho Chi Minh City and Hanoi is on display. Cruising down Ho Chi Minh's fashionable Dong Khoi Street or around Hanoi's Hoan Kiem Lake on a motorcycle and enjoying the more liberal atmosphere is now the done thing for the increasing ranks of middle class youth. Although *bia hoi* establishments exist in other large cities, they are most popular in Hanoi. These small, down-market bars cater exclusively to men – though there would be no objections to a Western woman sitting down for a drink – serving fresh beer at amazingly low prices. These bars are visited by all strata of Vietnamese society, from businessmen to cyclo-drivers, so they can be good places to meet the locals; but they usually run out of beer early and close by 8 or 9pm.

Karaoke bars are extremely popular with the Vietnamese. Ballroom dances like the waltz and mambo are still regularly practised at traditional dance halls. There are also increasing numbers of modern discos where locals and visitors dance to the latest international music.

SPORTS

Water Sports and Diving

With such an extensive coastline, Vietnam is quickly becoming a paradise for water sports enthusiasts. The best opportunities for **scuba diving** and **snorkelling** can be found in Hoi An, the Con Dao Archipelago and particularly Nha Trang, with Rainbow Divers (90A Hung Vuong; tel: 090-878 1756; www.divevietnam.com). Rainbow Divers has centres on Whale Island, Con Dao Island, and in Hoi An and Ho Chi Minh City. Numerous tour companies in Nha Trang also provide trips to nearby islands for snorkelling – one of the highlights of any trip to Nha Trang. The best conditions for diving and snorkelling are from June to September. Unfortunately diving conditions are not as pristine as they once where ten years ago, but diving supports a greater appreciation and understanding of the need to protect Vietnam's coral reefs.

Mui Ne is the **kite-boarding** and **wind-surfing** capital of Vietnam, with about a dozen kite centres along the beach. The most reputable centres include C2Sky Kite Center (Sunshine

Nha Trang is a major diving centre

Beach Resort, 82 Nguyen Dinh Chieu; tel: 091-665 5241; www.c2skykitecenter.com) and the old Storm Kiteboarding, now under management of Mia Resort (24 Nguyen Dinh Chieu; tel: 062-384 7442; www.mia-muine.com). November to April is the windy season in Mui Ne, and thus the optimum time for kite-boarding and wind-surfing.

Trekking

There are some opportunities for trekking in Vietnam, although at the moment not as many or as sophisticated as in nearby Thailand. Trekking tours can be organised at various travellers' cafés in Hanoi, Sapa and Dalat. From Sapa, treks to hill tribe village and Mount Fansipan are available. From Dalat, treks to waterfalls, hill tribe villages and overnight hikes in national parks can be arranged. These treks can often be combined with other activities such as repelling and mountain biking. Please note that due to political instability and government oppression of minorities in highlands areas, localities such as Dak Lak Province, Gia Lai Province, and Dien Bien Phu may be off-limits to trekking.

Cycling and Motorbiking

If you are prepared to put in the effort and venture off the beaten track, cycling can be a fantastic way to see the country. Vietnamese roads are by no means the best in the world and sometimes, especially during the rainy season, they can be terrible. While it is possible to cycle the length of Highway

One, from Hanoi to Ho Chi Minh City, it's far safer and enjoyable to concentrate on cycling in the countryside around Hue, Dalat or Hoi An and away from the big cities.

Bicycle and motorbike tours mainly depart from Dalat and lead down from the highlands to coastal cities. However, it is also possible to arrange and begin some tours from cities like Ho Chi Minh, Hanoi, Phan Thiet, Mui Ne, Nha Trang, Hoi An, Hue and Hanoi. In the case of motorbike tours, travellers normally ride as passengers, but it is possible to drive your own motorbike. Note that a helmet is required, as is a Vietnam driver's license, though the latter is usually only enforced in urban areas. In Dalat these tours can be arranged at tour offices; however it's also easy to simply approach the motorbike drivers above the Dalat Market, known as 'Easy Riders', and negotiate a custom tour and price.

Golf

Vietnam may not be the first the place you would think of for a golfing holiday in Asia, but there are some excellent courses dotted around the country. Probably the finest is the International Golf Club of Vietnam in Ho Chi Minh City. In Hanoi try the

Climbing Fansipan

At 3,143m (10,215ft) Mt Fansipan, Vietnam's highest peak, is only 10km (6 miles) from Sa Pa, but the terrain is difficult and the weather frequently bad. If you are considering scaling the summit, be aware that warm clothes, good boots, camping equipment and a guide are essential, as the round trip may take up to three days. You will also need to carry supplies, so it is best to make arrangements through a local trekking agency. For most of the climb the countryside is completely bereft of signs of humanity – you'll encounter just forest, monkeys, birds and fine mountain views.

Ho Tay theme park in Hanoi

King's Island Golf Club at Dong Mo Lake some 45km (28 miles) west of the city. At Phan Thiet is the challenging Ocean Dunes Golf Club (tel: 08-3824 3640), designed by Nick Faldo, while the hill resort of Dalat has the classy Dalat Palace Golf Club (tel: 063-3821 201) overlooking the majestic Xuan Huong Lake.

CHILDREN'S VIETNAM

On the whole Vietnam is a good destination for families with children. It's not so much that there are numerous and varied activities aimed specifically at children – there aren't. But the Vietnamese are good with children and will pay them a great deal of attention, especially if they are blonde and blue-eyed, in which case they seem as 'doll-like' to the Vietnamese as their petite, raven-haired children seem to Europeans and Americans.

There are zoos and amusement parks in both Hanoi and Ho Chi Minh City. The latter, in particular, has a good water park, while in Hanoi the water puppet shows are certain to amuse. Swimming opportunities and water sports are plentiful along the long central coast, though parents should pay attention to safety as facilities for this are very limited.

Food is not a problem as Vietnamese cuisine includes many mild rice and noodle dishes. Also, the French colonial legacy means familiar dishes from baguette and omelette to steak and *frites* are readily available in most towns and cities.

Calendar of Festivals

Most festivals in Vietnam follow the lunar calendar. In addition to the major nationwide celebrations, there are many smaller local festivals. Perhaps the best known of all Vietnamese festivals is Tet, marked for centuries by the explosion of a million firecrackers. Though these have been banned on grounds of safety, Tet is still a pretty noisy occasion.

January/February: Tet, 1st–3rd day of 1st lunar month. The biggest and most important celebration of the entire year, *Tet Nguyen Dan* (in full) heralds the start of the Vietnamese Lunar New Year. The most important days of Tet ('festival') are the first three days of the Lunar New year. The most interesting time for visitors is actually the week prior to the holiday, when night markets are filled with candy, flower and lantern vendors. Tet eve is celebrated with fireworks and dragon and lion dancing.

March/April: Holiday of the Dead, 5th day of the 3rd lunar month. On this family holiday many people visit the graves of their ancestors to tend them and make offerings of fruit, incense and paper money.

May/June: *Phat Dan*, 8th day of the 4th lunar month. Buddha's rites of passage are celebrated in pagodas, temples and homes. In some cities there are grand parades with lantern floats and dragon dancing held late in the evening.

Tet Doan Ngo (Summer Solstice Day), 5th day of the 5th lunar month. This Tet includes festivities to ensure good health and well-being. Offerings are made to spirits, ghosts and the god of death; all to ward off summer epidemics and plagues.

Trang Nguyen (Wandering Souls Day), 15th day of the 7th lunar month. This is the second most important Vietnamese festival. Graves are cleaned and offerings are made in homes and pagodas for the wandering souls of the forgotten dead.

September/October: *Tet Trung Thu* (Mid-Autumn Festival), 15th day of the 8th lunar month. Children parade around with candle-illuminated lanterns, and delicious pastry-covered 'mooncakes' with sweet lotus seed or red bean paste are eaten.

EATING OUT

Vietnamese cuisine is considered among the world's best. It's generally healthy, being high in fibre and fresh fruits and vegetables. It's tasty, it's inventive, and it's increasingly based on high-quality ingredients as the country grows more prosperous. Visitors have a wide choice of eating-places – roadside stalls and western-style cafés, expat-run Italian, Indian and American restaurants, hotel restaurants (which are usually good quality), as well as Vietnamese restaurants serving traditional dishes.

Like so much else in Vietnam, the cuisine reflects long years of cultural exchange with China, Laos, Cambodia, France and, more recently, the US. As elsewhere in Southeast Asia, *com* or rice is the main staple, though bread – especially baguettes introduced by the French – is available everywhere. What's more, bread is always fresh, as it's baked daily. As elsewhere in Southeast Asia, dishes are generally served at the same time rather than by course, and eaten with long-grain rice, dipping sauces and a wide range of fresh herbs and vegetables. Meals are generally eaten with chopsticks or, occasionally with a spoon, knife and fork.

Local Ingredients

Vietnam's long coastline, innumerable rivers, canals and waterways provide an ample and varied supply of fresh fish and seafood all year round. Freshwater and sea fish, shellfish, crabs, octopuses, squids – just about anything that swims or lives in water, including amphibians such as frogs – are eaten as the main source of protein

Arrive early

It is best to arrive in Vietnamese restaurants, particularly the smaller ones, by noon for lunch and 5.30pm for dinner, as food can run out quickly. At restaurants where prices are not listed, you should always ask the price before ordering.

Vietnamese cuisine utilises the freshest ingredients

in delicious dishes such as *cha ca*, a barbecued fish made in Hanoi, and in minced fishcakes.

The Vietnamese have created literally hundreds of innovative dishes using pork, chicken and beef, sometimes combining meat together with fish and seafood. Whether boiled, barbecued, grilled, stewed or fried, Vietnamese cuisine skilfully blends numerous flavours, textures and influences. Presentation, too, is important, and a bowl or jug of fresh leaves and herbs set on the table is considered essential.

The fish sauce called *nuoc mam* is ubiquitous in Vietnamese cooking. Set on every table like salt in Western countries, *nuoc mam* is used as an ingredient in many dishes, but is also combined with other ingredients as a condiment called *nuoc cham*. The fish sauce has something of a pungent aroma and flavour that can take some getting used to, but it is a definite complement to the subtle flavours of Vietnamese cuisine. Manufactured in coastal cities, especially Phan Thiet, the fish sauce is made by fermenting anchovies and salt in large wooden or ceramic barrels for about six months.

A dipping sauce is served with starters and a variety of snack-type foods. Every domestic kitchen or restaurant has its own formula, but usually the sauce consists of chilli, lime juice, garlic, sugar and pepper.

Vietnamese cooks use many fresh herbs – lemon grass, basil, coriander, mint, parsley, *laksa* leaf – as well as garlic, lime and ginger. These ingredients lend the cuisine a subtlety of flavour that sets it apart from its neighbours.

Regional Variations

Cuisine varies considerably from one part of Vietnam to another. Generally, food in the north tends to be less spicy, using fewer spices and herbs and – as in neighbouring China – more monosodium glutamate or MSG. In the central part of the country around Hue and Danang, food is spicier and also includes creative vegetarian cooking, particularly in Hue, where there are many Buddhists who follow a meatless diet. These vegetarian dishes are often accompanied by, or cooked together with *gao nep*, or glutinous rice – a variety quite distinct from the more familiar long grain types, and closely related to the culinary traditions of neighbouring Laos and northeast Thailand.

Southern cooking, the variety most familiar to those who have eaten in Vietnamese restaurants in America, Australia or Europe, tends to be more flavoursome and varied than that of the north. Often the dishes contain the same ingredients, but they are prepared quite differently.

The south has one essential advantage that helps to explain this: because of the warmer climate there is a much wider variety of fresh fruits and vegetables, including tropical delicacies such as custard apple, sapodilla, durian, pineapple, star fruit, dragon fruit, rambutan and mango. Numerous southern delicacies are served with raw, leafy vegetables, bean sprouts and herbs and wrapped up at table by the diner just before eating. This custom is probably indigenous to the area.

The southerners, living in a tropical area, also use more coconut milk in their cooking and create interesting dishes that combine sweet and sour flavours. The influence of Hoa or Chinese culinary traditions from Fujian, Hainan and Guangdong is also more apparent in the south, especially in Cholon and throughout the Mekong Delta.

Popular Dishes

Some of the more popular Vietnamese dishes include *cha gio* (known as *nem Saigon* in the north): small spring rolls of minced pork, shrimp, crabmeat, fragrant mushrooms and vegetables wrapped in thin rice paper and then deep-fried. *Cha gio*

A typical Vietnamese meal comprises a variety of small dishes served with noodles or rice

is rolled in a lettuce leaf with fresh mint and other herbs, then dipped in a sweet sauce.

Another dish eaten in a similar fashion is *cuon diep*, or shrimp, noodles, mint, coriander and pork wrapped in lettuce leaves. Hue, a city associated with Buddhism, is famous for its vegetarian cuisine and for its *banh khoai*, or 'Hue potato pancake'. A batter of rice flour and corn is fried with egg to make a pancake, then wrapped around pork or shrimp, onion, bean sprouts and mushrooms. Another Hue speciality is bun bo, or fried beef and noodles served with coriander, onion, garlic, cucumber, chilli peppers and tomato paste.

The small but ancient city of Hoi An is also famous for its local specialities. These include *coa lau*, a rice noodle soup said to be based on the Japanese soba tradition, served with slices of lean pork, soy sauce and fresh lime juice. This is usually topped with crumbled *banh da* or rice crackers. Other local Hoi An specialities include fried won ton dumplings, the simple but delicious *com ga* (chicken rice), and the enduringly popular 'white rose', or steamed shrimps wrapped in rice paper.

Other delicious dishes which exemplify Vietnamese cooking include *cha lua* – pork paté wrapped in banana leaves before cooking and served in baguettes as a popular streetside snack – and *chao tom*, a delicious and popular Hanoi speciality made from minced shrimp baked on sugar cane. The shrimp is removed from the sugar cane and rolled in rice paper with lettuce, cucumber, coriander and mint, and dipped in *nuoc cham* sauce.

Pho ga, a popular chicken variant of the national *pho bo* (rice noodle and beef soup) is particularly delicious. Available just about everywhere, *goi ga* is shredded chicken marinated in onion, vinegar, mint and, sometimes, peanuts – best eaten with white, long-grain rice. *Ga xao sa ot* is sautéed chicken cooked with lemongrass, fish sauce, garlic, onion and chillies. Sometimes peanuts are added.

Che is a popular dessert item sold early in the morning in most food markets, or after dark on street-side stands. Served hot or cold, it comes in many varieties as tasty mixtures of candied fruit, beans, corn and rice. Some kinds of this Vietnamese version of pudding also use tapioca, potato or even fungus.

Soups for All Seasons

Soups are popular throughout the country, and served with almost every meal. The best known soup dish, often eaten for breakfast or as a late-night snack, is *pho* (pronounced 'foh'), a broth of rice noodles topped with beef or chicken, fresh herbs and onion. Egg yolk is often added, as may be lime juice, chilli peppers or vinegar. Pho is often served with *quay* – a fried piece of flour dough. Northerners often say that southern *pho* is too sweet, while southerners claim the northern variant is too bland – yet both agree *pho* is the veritable stuff of life.

Another type of noodle dish, mostly popular in the

Pho ga is a popular dish across Vietnam

Cha gio spring rolls

south, is *mien ga* – a soup of chicken, coriander, fish sauce and spring onions. *Canh chua* is a sour soup generally served with shrimp or fish head; the stock is a fragrant blend of sweet and tangy flavours, using tomato, pineapple, star fruit, bean sprouts, fried onion, bamboo shoots, coriander, cinnamon and, naturally, nuoc mam. *Hu tieu nam vang* is chicken, beef, pork and shrimp served with a broth over rice noodles mixed with crabmeat, peanuts, onion and garlic.

Lau is the Vietnamese version of Chinese hotpot, but not nearly as spicy. It comes in many varieties, and is a favourite meal for large gatherings. *Lau hai san*, or seafood hotpot, reigns supreme along the coast. *Lau ca* and *lau bo* (fish and beef hotpot) are common inland. *Lau de* (goat hotpot) is a speciality in Binh Thuan and Ninh Thuan provinces.

What to Drink

Bottled fresh water, canned and bottled soft drinks and beers are available throughout the country. The range of beers, in particular, is extensive, with most large cities having at least one brand of their own. A number of foreign beer makers have set up operations in Vietnam and are steadily improving the quality of beers on offer. Most bottled beers are rather light and unremarkable. Draught beer is becoming increasingly available in large restaurants and micro-breweries. An unusual Vietnamese institution is *bia hoi*, or 'fresh beer', a concept first introduced by the Czechs but now beloved of beer-drinkers all over the country. Beer is delivered fresh daily in small tanker-trucks. *Bia hoi* establishments are usually very basic, but they are good places to meet the locals and the price is extraordinarily low – somewhere around 5000 dong or 25 US cents for a large glass.

French and Australian wines are increasingly popular, especially at restaurants in Hanoi, Ho Chi Minh City and other large cities. Locally produced wine is also available, made from grapes grown at the extensive vineyards near Phan Thiet and Phan Rang and bottled in Dalat. Vang Dalat (the name is an approximation of the French *vin*) is reasonably priced, although of dubious quality. The red is preferable to the white, which should only be attempted when very cold. Local rice liquors are cheap and fierce.

A wide variety of fresh fruit juices and smoothies are available. One unusual variant is dragon fruit – a magenta-coloured fruit whose white flesh is speckled with black seeds. All over the country, especially in the centre and the south, are *sinh to* stalls, easily recognised by their glass cases displaying a variety of colourful fruits and vegetables. Point to a selection of fruit and you will receive a liquidised fruit-and-ice shake, prepared with or without sugar (*duong*) as you prefer.

A Hanoi bar

Chinese tea, both hot and cold, is served everywhere, while Vietnamese coffee, which is grown in the Central Highlands and served with tiny individual metal filters, is delicious.

Vietnamese cuisine is characterised by subtle flavours.

TO HELP YOU ORDER...

restaurant	**nha hang**
Do you have an English menu?	**Ban co thuc don bang tieng Anh khong?**
Not too spicy, please.	**Lam on dung cho cay qua.**
I'm a vegetarian.	**Toi an chay.**
I'd like something to drink.	**Lam on cho phan giai khat.**
Please may I have the bill.	**Lam on tinh tien.**

...AND READ THE MENU

banh mi	bread	**rau song**	vegetables
ca	fish	**thit bo**	beef
ca phe	coffee	**thit heo**	pork
com	rice	**tom to**	prawn
ga	chicken	**tra**	tea
muc	squid	**trung**	egg
nuoc suoi	water	**vit**	duck

PLACES TO EAT

Prices given are for an average main dish for one person.

$$$ over US$20   **$$** US$10–20
$ under US$10

HANOI

Au Lac Do Brazil $$$ *6A Cao Ba Quat, tel: (04) 3845 5224, www. aulacdobrazil.com.* This all-you-can-eat Brazilian barbecue is a little unusual for Vietnam, though there are now three outlets.

Restaurant Bobby Chinn $$$ *77 Xuan Dieu Street; tel: (04) 3719 2460, www.bobbychinn.com; daily 11am–midnight.* Run by restaurateur, chef and Discovery Channel host Bobby Chinn, this long-established restaurant and lounge serves up unique Asian-Californian dishes in a funky yet refined dining area.

Bun Cha $ *20 Ta Hien. Bun cha* is seasoned and grilled pork pieces served with fresh rice noodles and drenched with a piquant sweet and sour sauce. This small streetside restaurant in the Old Quarter serves some of the best *bun cha* in town.

Cha Ca La Vong $ *14 Cha Ca, tel: (04) 3825 3929.* One of Hanoi's most famous dishes, *cha ca* is the only thing served here – fish grilled on a clay brazier at your table – with rice noodles, peanuts and herbs.

Green Tangerine $$$ *48 Hang Be, tel: (04) 3825 1286.* Located in a gorgeous restored French villa in the heart of the Old Quarter. Lounge in the atmospheric interior, or dine in the garden courtyard. The French chef creates mouthwatering international fusion and traditional French cuisine.

Highway 4 Bar & Restaurant $$ *5 Hang Tre, tel: (04) 3926 0639, www.highway4.com.* Specialises in exotic rice wine liquors and North Vietnamese cuisine, especially hotpot, fish, spring rolls and caramelised clay pot dishes.

La $$ *25 Ly Quoc Su, tel: (04) 3928 8933.* Tall wooden double-doors open to a casual bistro run by friendly and knowledgeable staff. The menu is a mix of western tastes and Asian fusion.

Le Tonkin $$ *14 Ngo Van So. tel: (04) 3943 3457.* Set in a century-old restored French villa, filled with regional antiquities and ambience. Vietnamese cuisine is modified to suit Westerners. Evening traditional music performances on Mondays and Fridays.

Quan An Ngon $$ *18 Phan Boi Chau, tel: (04) 3942 8162.* Sit at simple tables set in a pretty alfresco villa courtyard and enjoy traditional Vietnamese dishes served from the surrounding mock street food stalls. The restaurant can get very busy.

SA PA

Auberge Dang Truong $$ *7 Rue Muong Hoa, Sapa, tel: 020 387-1243.* This guesthouse has a restaurant on a terrace overlooking the owner's delightful garden. Delicious snacks and mains (both Vietnamese and Western), with a nice selection of vegetarian options.

Baguette & Chocolat $$ *Thac Bac Street, Sapa, tel: 020 387-1766, www.hoasuaschool.com.* The ground floor of this guesthouse is a quaint restaurant and café, with a bakery attached. Great cakes and pastries, plus you can order a packed picnic lunch if you're heading out on a trek.

HO CHI MINH CITY

Barbecue Garden $$ *135A Nam Ky Khoi Nghia, tel: (08) 3823 3340, www.barbecuegarden.com.* Clay pots with coals are set on each table so that you can barbecue your own skewered meats (pork, beef, chicken and seafood) and vegetables.

Ben Thanh Night Market $ *Phan Boi Chau and Phan Chu Trinh streets.* Post-dusk, open-air, makeshift eateries assemble outside Ben Thanh Market and serve a huge selection of good value, Vietnamese fare.

Black Cat $ *13 Phan Van Dat, tel: (08) 3829 2055*. Recognized by CNN as one of the best burgers in the world, Black Cat is a sanctuary of Western comfort food. The menu includes burgers, pizza, Indian, Tex-Mex and their famous fruit shakes.

Com Nieu Saigon $$ *6C Tu Xuong, tel: (08) 3932 6388*. Com Nieu is popular for its flavoursome southern cuisine and entertaining spectacle of waiters smashing clay pots of charcoal-grilled rice and throwing dishes across the room.

Quan An Ngon $ *138 Nam Ky Khoi Nghia, tel: (08) 3825 7179*. Quang An Ngon is popular with both local Vietnamese and expats. At around 5pm folding tables and chairs roll out onto the sidewalk to create a temporary smorgasbord of Vietnamese seafood and popular cuisine with ice-cold beer.

The Refinery $$ *74 Hai Ba Trung, tel: (08) 3823 0509*. This period French-style bistro is housed in a restored opium refinery, set off the street behind the Opera House. The menu is contemporary European and includes homemade ice-creams.

Paris Deli $ *31 Dong Khoi*. This is a French-style bistro located in the heart of Ho Chi Minh City's central shopping district. Come here when you're in the mood for delicious pastries and sandwiches and a relaxed atmosphere.

Square One $$$ *Mezzanine, Park Hyatt Saigon, 2 Lam Son Square, tel: (08) 3520 2357, www.saigon.park.hyatt.com*. The menu includes simple yet top-notch Western and Vietnamese dishes that are grilled, steamed and wok-fried in front of diners.

Tib $$ *187 Hai Ba Trung, Cholon, tel: (08) 3829 7242, www.tibrestaurant.com*. This cavernous restaurant specialises in authentic imperial Hue cuisine, like tiny rice pancakes with shredded shrimp. Decorated in traditional imperial style and set in a colonial villa. Reservations are essential.

Xu $$$ *Restaurant-Lounge 71–75 Hai Ba Trung, tel: (08) 3824 8468, www.xusaigon.com*. The ultra-sleek Xu serves up contemporary

Vietnamese fusion cuisine, true to its roots yet with an unmistakeable international twist apparent in dishes like tuna spring rolls with mango salsa. The menu also includes traditional Vietnamese and Western dishes.

NHA TRANG

Da Fernando $$ *96 Nguyen Thien Thuat, tel: (058) 352 8034.* The menu includes popular favourites like pizza, pasta, risotto and gnocchi, along with a few creative surprises. Sun-dried tomatoes and anchovies are Fernando's signature ingredients.

La Mancha $ *78 Nguyen Thien Thuat St, tel: (058) 352 7978.* This excellent tapas restaurant has a great atmosphere, lively Spanish music and a fountain at the centre. Complimentary fresh bread is served throughout the meal. Try the stewed Spanish sausages.

Louisiane Brewhouse $$ *Lot 29, Tran Phu, tel: (058) 352 1948, www.louisianebrewhouse.com.vn.* This beachside restaurant with swimming pool serves Vietnamese seafood, steaks, pizza and burgers, with sushi thrown in for variety. Try their home-brewed ginger ale with lemon grass.

Rainbow Divers $ *90A Hung Vuong, tel: (058) 352 4351, www.divevietnam.com.* The menu includes burgers, pizza, Australian meat pies, English fish and chips and New Zealand ice cream. The snug natural-wood interior feels like the cabin of a ship.

Sailing Club $$$ *72–74 Tran Phu, tel: (058) 382 6528.* One of the most happening places on Nha Trang's beach. The menu includes everything from sushi to tandoori.

Truc Linh I $$ *11 Biet Thu, tel: (058) 352 6742.* The Truc Linh eateries are popular seafood venues, where the catch of the day is displayed in enormous tanks on the street. These large, lively restaurants are busy into the night and also serve a wide range of backpacker favourites for non-seafood lovers.

HUE

Club Garden $ *8 Vo Thi Sau, tel: (054) 382 6327.* Come for the good seafood and the atmosphere in this elegant and friendly little family-run restaurant.

Dong Tam $ *48 Le Loi.* A good spot for a vegetarian lunch in the garden courtyard of a Buddhist family home. The menu is rather limited but prices are cheap and the set menus are good value.

JASS Japanese Restaurant $$ *12 Chu Van An, tel: (054) 382 8177.* The menu is small but the dishes are near-perfect, with flavours that are clean and delicate. The Japanese Associate of Supporting Streetchildren (JASS), runs an excellent programme to house, educate and train disadvantaged youth.

La Boulangerie Francaise $ *46 Nguyen Tri Phuong, tel: (054) 383 7437.* One of the finest French bakeries in the country. The tarts, pastries, fresh breads and cakes are all excellent.

Ngu Ha $$ *181 Xuan 68, tel: (054) 351 3320.* An ancient Hue house is the refined traditional royal cuisine, with Hue music too.

HOI AN

Cao Lau $ *296 Cua Dai.* This is a morning sidewalk stand located down an alley. It serves *cao lau*, *bun cary* and *Mi Quang* (rather dry and bland rice noodle specialty of Danang).

Ganesh Indian Restaurant $$ *24 Tran Hung Dao, tel: (0510) 386 4538.* Lots of tandoori, curry and vegetarian choices. Located just north of the Old Town so you can drive or walk from most hotels.

Mango Rooms $$ *111 Nguyen Thai Hoc St, tel: (0510) 391 0839, www.mangorooms.com.* A bright and breezy place that serves an inventive Vietnamese menu. The Vietnamese chef grew up in the US and gives a decidedly Californian spin to the dishes.

Morning Glory $ *106 Nguyen Thai Hoc, tel: (0510) 224 1555, www.hoianhospitality.com.* A cosy restaurant for Vietnamese street food, housed in an elegant old French colonial villa in the middle of the historic quarter. There is also a good cookery school here.

DALAT

Café de la Poste $$ *Tran Phu Street, tel: (063) 382 5444.* A charming French café behind the Dalat Palace Hotel, serving sandwiches, pasta, French and Asian dishes. Excellent breakfast buffets.

Da Quy $ *49D Truong Cong Dinh, tel: (063) 351 0883.* Da Quy is a popular restaurant for local Vietnamese dishes. Service is friendly and attentive, and prices are cheap (in the range of street food). Try the clay pot dishes, barbecue meats and Vietnamese deserts.

Tu An's Peace Café $ *57 Truong Cong Dinh, tel: (063) 351 1524.* Both the Vietnamese and foreign food is great. Try the goulash, pasta or simply ask for whatever you want and she can usually make it.

MUI NE

The Champa Restaurant $$$ *Coco Beach Resort, 58 Nguyen Dinh Chieu.* Champa has some of the finest food in Mui Ne, serving French 'cuisine bourgeois'. The restaurant is decorated with Cham art and the large terrace overlooks the gardens and pool. The bar serves Cuban cigars and great cocktails, accompanied by classy French tunes.

Forest Restaurant (Rung) $$ *67 Nguyen Dinh Chieu, tel: (062) 384 7589, www.forestrestaurant.com.* Elegant Vietnamese dining in a garden setting. The interior is immaculately decorated with rare highland crafts and artefacts.

Vietnam Home $ *125A, B Nguyen Dinh Chieu, tel: (062) 384-7687.* Set in an atmospheric bamboo treehouse of sorts, Vietnam Home offers a varied menu of local favourites and regional specialties. The food is top-notch at reasonable prices. Occasionally there is a live band; either ethnic Cham or highlands music.

A–Z TRAVEL TIPS

A Summary of Practical Information

A

ACCOMMODATION

The standard of Vietnamese accommodation has come a long way in the last few years, and you will find international standard hotels in most of the larger cities. Ho Chi Minh City offers the widest range of top quality hotels, but Hanoi is catching up fast. Accommodation in Vietnam commonly includes large 4- and 5-star hotels, and resorts all the way down to small, family-run guesthouses.

Generally the number of rooms available at any time far outstrips the demand – with the notable exception of Hoi An, or in the high season; Hanoi, Ho Chi Minh City and Mui Ne. During low season, some resorts close for renovations. Discounts are possible.

hotel	**khach san**
guesthouse	**nha khach/nha nghi/nha tro**
I'd like a single/double room with bathroom.	**Toi muon mot phong chiec/doi phong tam.**
What's the rate per night?	**Mot dem bao nhieu?**

AIRPORTS

Vietnam has three international airports, Hanoi's Noi Bai airport, Ho Chi Minh City's Tan Son Nhat and Danang International Airport.

Tan Son Nhat Airport (SGN; tel: (08) 3844 6662, www.hochiminhcityairport.com), the busiest of the three, is located 7km (4 miles) or 15 minutes northeast of downtown Ho Chi Minh City. Metered taxis are available and far better organised than in Hanoi. The fare from downtown Ho Chi Minh City should be about 150,000 dong (US$9).

Noi Bai Airport (HAN; tel: (04) 3827 1513, www.hanoiairportonline.com) is 35km (22 miles) north of Hanoi. Vietnam Airlines provides a shuttle bus service to and from Pho Quang Trung, the central Hanoi booking office, for 70,000 dong (US$4) per person. Taxis are available in front of the terminal building and a typical fare to anywhere in downtown Hanoi would be US$20.

Danang International Airport (DAD; tel: 0511 382-3377, www.danangairportonline.com) is 2km (1.2 miles) west of the town and has been developed as a regional airline entry point.

B

BICYCLE AND MOTORBIKE HIRE (RENTAL)

Bicycles can be hired from various cafés, travel agents and hotels in Hanoi and Ho Chi Minh City. For the Imperial City of Hue a bicycle is the perfect way to see the sights. In recent years more and more cyclists have taken to touring the country on mountain bikes. Most buses and trains will allow bicycles on board and there are bicycle repair shops in most towns.

Motorbike hire is possible in all cities and most resorts, cafés, travel agents and hotels, but for getting around Ho Chi Minh City and Hanoi it's only a good idea if you have some previous experience. The traffic in Hanoi is overwhelming, though slow, and does not appear to follow any road rules. In Ho Chi Minh City, the streets are wider and things move at a much quicker pace, so great care is needed.

Where can I hire a bicycle?	**Toi co the muon xe dap o dau?**
Where can I hire a motorbike?	**Toi co the muon xe mo to o dau?**

BUDGETING FOR YOUR TRIP

Hanoi and Ho Chi Minh City are not expensive when compared with other international cities, though they are the most expensive localities in Vietnam. Most prices are flexible, so be sure to haggle, and settle on a price before you use the service. Shop away from tourist areas, toward the back or markets, and in smaller towns for the best prices. Eat street food and in restaurants away from hotels. Always pay in Vietnamese currency to avoid being cheated on the exchange rate, and be wary of strangers who offer to help you get a better rate; they probably get a commission.

C

CAR HIRE (RENTAL)

It is not possible for tourists to legally drive a car in Vietnam due to the logistics and time involved in getting a local driver's license. Hiring a car and driver can be a convenient way to see the country however, expect to pay up to $100 per day.

Where can I hire a car?	**Toi co the muon xe hoi o dau?**
How much is the daily rate?	**Gia bao nhieu tien mot ngay?**
How much is the weekly rate?	**Gia bao nhieu tien mot tuan?**
Is insurance included?	**Co bao gom bao hiem?**

CLIMATE

The climate in the north is influenced by cold air from China, and from November to April northern Vietnam experiences a relatively cool and humid winter. In the mountains temperatures fall as low as freezing point. Between May and October, temperatures rise, coupled with heavy rain and sometimes typhoons. Both the north and centre's hottest months are June, July and August.

Southern Vietnam's climate is characterised by relatively constant temperatures, a season of heavy rains between May and October, a relatively dry season from November to February, and a hot season between February and April when temperatures may reach 35°C (95°F). The rains are usually heavy and conditions during this period can be sticky and uncomfortable.

Hanoi is generally cooler than Ho Chi Minh City and is prone to greater temperature extremes (8–33°C/46–91°F). Ho Chi Minh City is hot most of the year (21–36°C/70–97°F). The Hai Van Pass just north of Danang acts as a climatic barrier between north and south. Hue and Danang may be only about 3 hours' drive apart, but the former is decidedly colder, especially in winter.

CLOTHING

In the cool season the north of the country, especially the mountains around Sa Pa, can be quite cold, so pack a sweater. The sun can be very fierce so a sun hat is advisable. Generally loose cotton clothes are recommended. It's also a good idea to keep a cheap plastic raincoat in your travelling bag. On the whole Vietnam is a relaxed country when it comes to dress, although monks prefer people not to wear T-shirts and shorts when visiting temples and other holy sites. It is customary to remove shoes when entering a temple or visiting someone's home, so bring easily removable footwear.

CRIME AND SAFETY

Compared to many countries Vietnam is a remarkably safe place to visit and you are unlikely to have serious problems. Bag and mobile phone snatchers can be a problem in Ho Chi Minh City, Hanoi and Nha Trang, especially around the tourist areas at night. When walking or travelling in a cyclo, keep one hand firmly on your handbag or camera. Be wary of friendly strangers (usually Filipino mafia) approaching you in HCMC, or other heavily touristed areas and inviting you to their home. An elaborate gambling scam begins this way. Victims have been drugged and robbed. Unfortunately foreigners are largely on their own when they are victims of crime in Vietnam. Try to file a report at the police station or seek assistance from your embassy if necessary.

I want to report a theft.	**Toi muon bao cao mot vu pham phap.**
My handbag/wallet/ticket has been stolen.	**Tui xach/Vi tien/Ve cua toi da bi an cap.**
My passport has been stolen.	**Ho Chieu cua toi da bi an cap.**
Help! Thief!	**Giup toi! Ke an cap!**

D

DRIVING

Vietnamese officially drive on the right. Road etiquette is lax and conditions can be chaotic. Both Hanoi and Ho Chi Minh City's streets are clogged with traffic. An excessive use of the horn is all too common, while speed limits are often unmarked and other signposting is erratic.

If you hire a motorbike, take great care and avoid riding at night due to the danger from poorly lit vehicles, livestock and potholes on country roads.

stop	**ngung**
no entry	**cam vao**
no parking	**cam dau**
one way	**mot chieu**
danger	**nguy hiem**
speed limit	**to do gioi han**
turn left/right	**queo sang trai/sang phai**
Fill the tank, please.	**Lam on do day binh.**
petrol	**xang**
leaded	**co chat chi**
unleaded	**khong co chi**

E

ELECTRICITY

Electricity is rated at 220 volts, although you may still find the odd place rated at 110 volts. Sockets are of the European or American type (two-pin; both round and flat prongs are equally common).

EMBASSIES AND CONSULATES

Embassies in Hanoi:

Australia: 8 Dao Tan Street; tel: (04) 3831 7755; www.vietnam.embassy.gov.au.

Canada: 31 Hung Vuong Street; tel: (04) 3734 5000; www.canadain-ternationalgc.ca/vietnam.

Ireland: Floor 8, Tower B, Vincom City Towers, 191 Ba Trieu, tel: (04) 3974 3291.

New Zealand: 63 Ly Thai To Street; tel: (04) 3824 1481; www.nzembassy.com.

South Africa: 3rd Floor, Central Building, 31 Hai Ba Trung, tel: (04) 3936 2000.

UK: Central Building, 31 Hai Ba Trung Street; tel: (04) 3936 0500; http://ukinvietnam.fco.gov.uk/en.

US: 7 Lang Ha Street; tel: (04) 3831 4590; http://vietnam.usembassy.gov.

Consulates in Ho Chi Minh City:

Australia: 5b Ton Duc Thang Street, District 1; tel: (08) 3829 6035; www.hcmc.vietnam.embassy.gov.au.

Canada: 235 Dong Khoi Street, District 1; tel: (08) 3827 9899.

UK: 25 Le Duan Street, District 1; tel: (08) 3829 8433.

US: 4 Le Duan Street, District 1; tel: (08) 3822 9433.

EMERGENCIES

For all emergencies in Vietnam ring 116. Other numbers include 113 (Police) and 114 (Fire). For directory enquiries ring 116.

G

GAY AND LESBIAN TRAVELLERS

On the whole homosexuality is tolerated in Vietnam, although not embraced as in Thailand. The gay scene is in evidence most notably in Hanoi and Ho Chi Minh City where there's an active café society.

GETTING THERE

By air. There are a number of ways to reach Vietnam, but the usual, and easiest, is by air. Because of the variety of fares available it is best to contact an experienced travel agent before leaving home. Some of the cheaper air tickets need to be booked well in advance.

A number of international airlines fly to Vietnam with direct daily flights from Bangkok, Hong Kong, Kuala Lumpur, Phnom Penh and Singapore. United Airlines now has a direct flight to Ho Chi Minh City from San Francisco via Hong Kong. Other direct flights to Hanoi's Noi Bai airport include Dubai, Guangzhou, Kunming, Moscow, Paris, Seoul, Taipei, Tokyo and Vientiane. Ho Chi Minh City's Tan Son Nhat airport has direct links with Dubai, Manila, Melbourne, Osaka, Paris, Seoul, Siem Reap, Sydney, and Taipei. It is advisable to reconfirm all your flights 72 hours before take-off.

Key Airline Offices in HCMC

Air Asia, www.airasia.com
Air France, www.airfrance.com.vn
Bangkok Air, www.bangkokair.com
British Airways, www.ba.com
Cathay Pacific, www.cathaypacific.com
Emirates Airlines, www.emirates.com
KLM Royal Dutch Airlines, www.klm.com
Lufthansa, www.lufthansa.com

Malaysia Airlines, www.malaysiaairlines.com
Qantas, www.qantas.com
Singapore Airlines, www.singaporeair.com
Thai Airways, www.thaiairvn.com
Tiger Airways, www.tigerairways.com
United Airlines, www.unitedairlines.com.vn
Vietnam Airlines, www.vietnamairlines.com

By road. It's possible to enter Vietnam by land at a number of border crossings. From Cambodia there are three main crossing points: Chau Doc, Vinh Xuong and Moc Bai. From Laos: Lao Bao, Cau Treo, Nam Can, Cha Lo, Na Meo, and Bo Y. From China: Lao Cai, Dong Dang and Mong Cai.

By river. It's now possible to enter Vietnam by riverboat from Cambodia. Ferries leave Phnom Penh via the Bassac River or Lower Mekong (which becomes the Song Hau Giang in Vietnam). The border entry point is at Chau Doc in the Mekong Delta.

GUIDES AND TOURS

A number of excellent travel agencies operate in Hanoi and Ho Chi Minh City offering tours and guides to all parts of the country. Of particular use are:

Buffalo Tours, 94 Ma May Street, Hanoi; tel: (04) 3828 0702, www. buffalotours.com. Very good for adventure tours and trips into the mountainous north.

Handspan Adventure Travel, 78 Ma May Street, Hanoi; tel: 04-3926 2828, www.handspan.com. Established in 1997, this young adventure travel company offers excellent value-for-money tours such as kayaking, mountain biking, trekking and cruising, with experienced guides and an environmentally-sensitive focus.

SinhBalo Adventures, 283/20 Pham Ngu Lao, District 1, Ho Chi Minh City; tel: (08) 3837 6766, www.sinhbalo.com. This was set up by Le Van Sinh, one of Vietnam's original tour operators and owner of the famed Sinh Café.

H

HEALTH AND MEDICAL CARE

Immunisation is recommended against cholera, typhoid, tetanus and hepatitis. Always drink bottled water, which is widely available, never tap water. Most will want to avoid drinks with ice sold on the street. Avoid eating raw vegetables and fruit without thoroughly washing and peeling them yourself.

Malaria risk exists in the whole country, excluding urban centres, the Red River delta and the coastal plains. High-risk areas include central highlands and the western parts of the coastal provinces. Consult your doctor about malaria prophylaxis and bring along some good mosquito repellent for use on exposed skin at night. After dark it is advisable to wear long-sleeved shirts and long trousers. Dengue fever is a risk in all areas of the country, including cities.

For medical attention in Hanoi, try the **Vietnam-Korea Friendship Clinic**, 12 Chu Van An, Ba Dinh District; tel: (04) 3843 7231.

In Ho Chi Minh City try the **HCMC Family Medical Practice**, Diamond Plaza, 34 Le Duan; tel: (08) 3822 7848.

Where is a chemist?	**Nha thuoc tay o dau?**
Where is a doctor?	**Bac si o dau?**
Where is a dentist?	**Nha si o dau?**
sunburn/sunstroke	**chay nang**
an upset stomach	**dau bung**

L

LANGUAGE

Vietnamese is spoken by virtually the entire population. Today's Vietnamese is tonal and this has been acquired over the centuries mainly from neighbouring Tai-speaking peoples. The Chinese element, which is also tonal, consists of an extensive vocabulary, especially in the realms of philosophy, literature and administration.

Monday	**thu hai**	Friday	**thu sau**
Tuesday	**thu ba**	Saturday	**thu bay**
Wednesday	**thu tu**	Sunday	**chu nhat**
Thursday	**thu nam**		

Vietnamese is a challenging language to master and requires intensive study, but it is possible to learn some basic vocabulary and this will be much appreciated by the locals. Particularly useful are numbers, food and travel terms. With Vietnam's burgeoning tourist industry more and more young people are learning English and are only too pleased to get in some practice.

one	**mot**	eleven	**muoi mot**
two	**hai**	twelve	**muoi hai**
three	**ba**	thirteen	**muoi ba**
four	**bon**	fourteen	**muoi bon**
five	**nam**	twenty	**hai muoi**
six	**sau**	twenty-one	**hai muoi mot**
seven	**bay**	twenty-two	**hai muoi hai**
eight	**tam**	thirty	**ba muoi**
nine	**chin**	fifty	**nam muoi**
ten	**muoi**	ninety	**chin muoi**
100	**mot tram**	10,000	**muoi nghin**
200	**hai tram**	100,000	**tram nghin**
1,000	**mot nghin**	1,000,000	**mot trieu**

M

MAPS

Most local Vietnamese bookshops have excellent city and province maps, in both English and Vietnamese. One excellent map that is available in most good international bookstores is the *Insight Flexi Map: Vietnam, Cambodia & Laos*.

MEDIA

The best local English-language newspapers are the daily *Vietnam News* and weekly *Vietnam Investment Review*, and magazines like the monthly *Vietnam Economic Times* and *Vietnam Today*. These are targeted at foreign investors and their main purpose is to emphasise local investment opportunities. Popular English-language magazines include *The Word*, *Asia Life* and *East-West Traveler*.

MONEY

The unit of currency in Vietnam is called the dong, abbreviated d (1us$ = around 21,000 dong). US dollars are widely accepted everywhere, although you will receive more value for money if you pay in dong. Room rates are often quoted in dollars.

Theoretically most major currencies can be exchanged in Vietnam, but in reality it is better to bring us dollars. At the moment only certain travellers' cheques and credit cards are acceptable in the big cities. ATMs are widely available in most cities.

Where is a bank?	**Ngan hang o dau?**
I want to change...	**Toi muon doi...**
some money	**tien mat**
travellers' cheques	**sec du lich**
Can I pay with a credit	**Toi co the tra bang the tin**
card?	**dung duoc khong?**

O

OPENING TIMES

Government offices are usually open Mon–Fri 8am–11.30am and 2–5pm, and sometimes Sat 8am–noon. Museums are usually open Tue–Sun 8am–noon and 2–5pm, but it is advisable to check before a visit. Temples are generally open daily 6am–6pm.

Shops and supermarkets are mostly open daily from as early as 6am and close any time from 6–10pm. Banks are open Mon–Fri 8am–3pm, Sat 8am–noon. Banks, administrative offices and museums, but not post offices, are closed on all public holidays and occasionally on religious festivals.

P

POLICE

Conspicuous in their rather bright olive green uniforms, the police are not known for their friendly manner. Few will speak much English. If you do get something stolen and need a report for your insurance company, it's best to take an English-speaking Vietnamese along with you to the police station. The emergency number is 113.

POST OFFICES

Post offices are found in most towns and many have facilities for express mail services. The main post office in Hanoi is Buu Dien Ha Noi, 75 Dinh Tien Hoang Street; in Ho Chi Minh City, it's the Buu Dien Ho Chi Minh, next to Notre Dame Cathedral. Post offices are generally open every day 6am–8pm.

PUBLIC HOLIDAYS

There are a number of official public holidays on fixed dates:

1 January	New Year's Day
3 February	Communist Party of Vietnam Day

30 April	Liberation of Saigon
1 May	International Labour Day
19 May	Ho Chi Minh's Birthday
27 July	War Martyrs' Memorial Day
2 September	National Day
25 December	Christmas Day

Many of Vietnam's major holidays are tied to the lunar calendar and therefore vary from year to year:

January/February: *Tet Nguyen Dan* (Lunar New Year) or Tet for short is the most important festival of the year. Many people take a week off to celebrate, but officially the festival lasts three days.

January/February: *Dong Da* Day celebrates Vietnam's victory over the Chinese in 1789.

March/April: *Thanh Minh* (Holiday of the Dead) honours the dead. Families make trips to the graves of deceased relatives.

April/May: *Phat Dan* celebrates the Buddha's Birth, Enlightenment and Death. Buddhists visit temples, shrines and private homes.

June/July: *Trung Nguyen* (Wandering Soul's Day), the second most important festival. Offerings are made to the souls of the dead.

November/December: Confucius' Birthday.

R

RELIGION

Most Vietnamese describe themselves as Buddhists, though they practise a mix of Buddhism, Taoism, ancestor worship and Confucianism. The Cham of the central coast are largely Hindu, while those of the Mekong Delta tend to be Muslim. Indigenous Vietnamese religions include the wildly syncretic Cao Dai, with its centre at Tay Ninh in the south, and the modified Buddhist Hoa Hao, centred on Chau Doc in the Mekong Delta. Hill tribes have a wide variety of animist religions which may adopt aspects of Buddhism or Hinduism. There are significant numbers of Catholics and Protestants.

The latter are highly persecuted in rural areas, though worship more freely in the big cities. Christians lost most of their land to government confiscations, and many continue to protest for the return of their church property.

T

TELEPHONES

The country code for Vietnam is 84. The city code for Hanoi is 04, for Ho Chi Minh City 08. Other important area codes are as follows: Dalat 063; Danang 0511; Hoi An 0510; Halong 033; Hue 054; Mui Ne 062; Nha Trang 058. The leading 0 is dropped when making an international call to Vietnam.

To make an IDD call, dial the international prefix 00, followed by the country code, area code and the number. International calls can be made from most hotels, but call charges are very high – some of the most expensive in the world. The hotel will also add a hefty service charge. Calls can also be made from post offices. This is cheaper, but you will be charged for the first three minutes whether you use them or not. Reverse charges (collect calls) are not permitted.

I want to make a call to... **Toi muon goi dien cho...**

TIME ZONE

Vietnam is 7 hours ahead of GMT. There is no daylight savings time. The chart below shows the times in Vietnam and various other cities across the world.

New York	London	Jo'burg	**Vietnam**	Sydney	Auckland
Midnight	5am	6am	**noon**	2pm	4pm

TIPPING

Tipping was never a part of traditional Vietnamese culture, but these days it is appreciated. If you feel you have been well looked after, a small token of thanks would not be out of place. Most top hotels and restaurants will add a service charge to your bill. Tipping tour guides, waiters and car drivers is becoming more common.

| Is service (tip) included? | **Da tinh tien hau ban vao hoa don chua?** |

TOILETS

All hotels and restaurant that cater to foreign tourists have western style toilets and should have toilet paper… most of the time.

| Where are the toilets, please? | **Nha ve sinh o dau?** |

TOURIST INFORMATION

Vietnam has yet to develop a network of tourist information offices overseas, and quite frankly, even domestic tourism administration offices will be of no assistance to most travellers.

Within Vietnam, the state-run body that theoretically looks after visitors is **Vietnam National Administration of Tourism** (VNAT; www.vietnamtourism.com), with its head office at 80 Quan Su, Hanoi; tel: (04) 3942 1061; email: vnat@vietnam-tourism.com. It is, however, more involved in new hotel and infrastructure investments than providing tourist services. State-run 'tourist offices' under the VNAT (or local provincial organisations) are really profit-making tour agents and are not geared to tourist requirements. For tours, car hire, information, go to private-run tour agencies.

In contrast, another state organisation, Trung Tam Du Lich Thanh Nien Vietnam (Vietnam's Youth Tourism Centre), is very helpful and can organise tailor-made tours. Contact them at 270 Nguyen Dinh Chieu, District 3, Ho Chi Minh City; tel: (08) 3933 0281.

Where is the tourist office?   **Van phong huong dan khach du lich o dau?**

TRANSPORT

Taxis. All the large towns have taxi services and all vehicles are metered. Expect to pay at least a dollar for a direct ride across downtown (District 1) HCMC. In Hanoi try Airport Taxis (tel: (04) 3873 3333), Hanoi Taxis (tel: (04) 3853 5252) or Mai Linh Taxis (tel: (04) 3822 2666). For Ho Chi Minh City try Airport Taxis (tel: (08) 3844 6666), Mai Linh Taxis (tel: (08) 3826 2626) or Vina Taxis (tel: (08) 3811 1111). Beware that taxis, particularly at airports, are notorious for scamming tourists.

Cyclos. Though quite slow, the cyclo, or trishaw, can be a great way to get around most towns, if you have time on your hands. Many drivers, especially in Ho Chi Minh City, speak some English. Cyclos are technically banned in Hanoi and Ho Chi Minh City, so the driver will have to make certain detours.

Bus. Vietnam has an extensive bus network with dozens of unaffiliated operators, but travelling this way can be tiring. Large express buses travel between most of the major towns and cities. Unfortunately buses do tend to be overcrowded and prone to breakdowns. If you have to travel by bus it is best to make the journey in daylight hours as many vehicles travel without lights at night. Phuong Trang is one of the better operators though many different companies have offices in tourist areas.

Train. Vietnam's rather aged rail network stretches between Hanoi and Ho Chi Minh City. It is served daily by the Reunification Express that stops at many towns on the way. The journey between the two cities usually takes between 30 and 36 hours. It is a safer way to travel than the bus, but don't leave your belongings unattended, and bring a padlock with you. Food is available on the trains and a variety of snack vendors come aboard at stations. Air-conditioned sleepers are available between Hanoi and Ho Chi Minh City. From Hanoi there are rail links to the Chinese border at Lao Cai and Lang Son, and also to the port city of Haiphong. For further information on Vietnam's rail network, including train fares and timetables, check www.vr.com.vn/english.

Hanoi's main station is at 120 Le Duan Street; tel: (04) 3942 3697. Ho Chi Minh City's is at 1 Nguyen Thong Street; tel: (08) 3843 6528.

Boat. Several key locations are accessed by boat, including Halong Bay, Tam Coc, the Perfume Pagoda and the Mekong Delta. All such rides are atmospheric and both pleasant and memorable. Tour operators for Halong Bay include: Buffalo Tours (tel: (04) 3828 0702; www.buffalotours.com), Handspan Adventure Travel (tel: (04) 3926 2828; www.handspan.com) and Exotissimo (tel: (04) 3828 2150; www.exotissimo.com). For the Mekong Delta, see Cuu Long Tourist (tel: 070-382 3616; www.cuulongtourist.com), located on the ground floor of Cuu Long B Hotel at Number 1, 1 Thang 5 Street in Vinh Long.

Where is the bus stop?	**Tram xe buyt o dau?**
Where is the railway station?	**Ga xe lua o dau?**
When is the next bus for...?	**May gio thi chuyen xe buyt... se toi?**
When is the next train for...?	**May gio thi chuyen tau lua ... se toi?**
I want a ticket to...	**Toi muon dat truoc mot ve di...**
single (one-way)	**ve di mot chieu**
return (round trip)	**ve khu hoi**
Will you tell me when we get to...?	**Khi xe den ... ban co the bao ch o toi biet khong a?**

V

VISAS AND ENTRY REQUIREMENTS

With a few exceptions, a visa is essential for Vietnam. A single entry 30-day tourist visa can usually be processed in two to five working days and costs around US$30. Apply either through a travel agent (paying a small fee), or direct with a Vietnamese embassy or consulate. Bangkok and Phnom Penh are considered the easiest places to acquire visas – including multiple-entry business visas, which start at US$100, with no extra paperwork, but it should be fairly easy in major Western cities. For a list of Vietnamese foreign missions overseas, check www.mofa.gov.vn.

Some tour operators now offer visas on arrival: visas are granted upon presentation of a pre-arranged confirmation letter at a 'visa on arrival' desk at Hanoi Airport. Visas can be extended locally (usually by 30 days) at a cost of about us$30. Extensions are best processed by a local travel agent in either Ho Chi Minh City or Hanoi. Always make sure your passport is valid for at least another 6 months.

W

WEBSITES AND INTERNET ACCESS

Free Wi-fi is everywhere, and local SIM cards with 3G internet have some of the cheapest rates in the world.

For general news on the country try **www.tuoitrenews.vn**, **www.thanhniennews.com** and **http://english.vietnamnet.vn**.

For culture and entertainment articles try **www.wordhcmc.com** and **www.wordhanoi.com**.

For environmental issues, and to report trafficking of endangered species try **www.envietnam.org** and **www.wildlifeatrisk.org.**

For local stories and travel advice, visit **www.fisheggtree.com**, and **www.muinebeach.net**.

Recommended Hotels

Although Vietnam's hotel scene does not quite match up to nearby destinations like Hong Kong and Thailand, it is catching up fast, with growing tourist numbers fuelling a building boom. This is good news for visitors, who can often find a new place with smart rooms at competitive prices. Generally, though not exclusively, the large, state-run hotels are run by indifferent staff, while low and mid-range mini-hotels are often operated by families who will do all they can to make their guests happy.

Most places above US$20 include at least a basic breakfast, air conditioning, baths, satellite TV and minibar. Many hotels have good websites that can help you make a choice, and internet bookings often give cheaper rates. Reservations are not generally necessary, except during major festivals such as Tet.

Prices given below are for a double or twin room during high season, and most places will give considerable discounts during the low season.

$$$	over US$50
$$	US$15–50
$	under US$15

HANOI

Church Hotel $ *9 Nha Tho, tel: (04) 3928 8118, www.churchhotel. com.vn*. This gem of a boutique hotel, just steps away from St Joseph's Cathedral, was built in 2004 and features stylishly appointed rooms overlooking trendy Nha Tho Street and the Ba Da Pagoda.

De Syloia Hotel $$$ *17A Tran Hung Dao, tel: (04) 3824 5346, www. desyloia.com*. A small but pleasant boutique hotel just south of the Old Quarter, with an excellent restaurant and small but good gym facilities.

Hanoi Daewoo Hotel $$$ *360 Kim Ma, tel: (04) 3831 5555, www. hanoi-daewoohotel.com*. This immense complex in western Hanoi has every conceivable facility. Rooms are large, quiet and comfy.

Hanoi Elegance Hotel II $$ *85 Ma May, tel: (04) 3926 3451, www. hanoielegancehotel.com*. A stylish, modern hotel built in 2006 right in the heart of the Old Quarter. Large, airy, well-furnished rooms, and helpful English-speaking staff.

Hanoi Paradise Hotel $$ *53 Hang Chieu, tel: (04) 3929 0026, www. hanoiparadisehotel.com*. One of few Old Quarter hotels to boast a pool. Opened in 2006, all rooms have an internet-connected computer. Free bottle of red wine, fruits and flowers on arrival.

Hilton Hanoi Opera $$$ *1 Le Thanh Tong, tel: (04) 3933 0500, www. hanoi.hilton.com*. An architecturally impressive hotel built to complement the neighbouring Opera House. Rooms are large, airy and modern. The wide, spacious lobby features live music and free Wi-fi.

Hoa Binh Hotel $$$ *27 Ly Thuong Kiet, tel: (04) 3825 3692, www. hoabinhhotel.com*. A small and elegant hotel with a sweeping wooden staircase and lovely French colonial touches. Rooms facing the street can be noisy in the morning.

Intercontinental Westlake Hanoi $$$ *1 Nghi Tam, tel: (04) 6270 8888, www.intercontinental.com*. A luxurious new hotel built over the West Lake and overlooking an 800-year-old pagoda. The rooms are large, comfortable and elegantly outfitted, with hotel pool and gym.

Melia Hanoi $$$ *44B Ly Thuong Kiet, tel: (04) 3934 3343, www.meliahanoi.com*. Located in Hanoi's business and diplomatic district. On site are five excellent restaurants, bars, a deli and a pool. Also features a helipad on its rooftop and the largest pillarless ballroom in Vietnam.

Sheraton Hanoi Hotel $$$ *11 Xuan Dieu, tel: (04) 3719 9000, www. sheraton.com*. The lakeside swimming pool, floodlit tennis courts, conference facilities and staff are all excellent. The more expensive rooms have lake views.

Sofitel Legend Metropole Hanoi $$$ *15 Ngo Quyen, tel: (04) 3826 6919, www.sofitel-legend.com*. Built in 1901 and renovated by the

French Sofitel company in 2005, this grande dame has maintained its colonial-era atmosphere while improving on its comfort levels.

Sofitel Plaza Hanoi $$$ *1 Thanh Nien, tel: (04) 3823 8888, www. sofitelplazahanoi.com*. The 20-storey Sofitel Plaza dominates the skyline at the edge of West Lake and is home to the best indoor/outdoor swimming pool in the city.

HO CHI MINH CITY

Caravelle Hotel $$$ *19 Lam Son Square, tel: (08) 3823 4999, www. caravellehotel.com*. The 5-star Caravelle is one of the city's most celebrated hotels. A glitzy 24-floor edifice, the original low-rise wing was famously home to foreign press corps during the Vietnam War.

Hotel Continental Saigon $$$ *132–134 Dong Khoi, tel: (08) 3829 9201, www.continentalvietnam.com*. The antithesis of HCMC's slick and modern downtown hotels, the charming, historic Continental has a to-die-for location. Today state-run, this 1880s colonial-era hotel seems hardly changed since Graham Greene was holed up in Room 214.

Elios $$ *233 Pham Ngu Lao, tel: (08) 3838 5585, www.elioshotel.vn*. Located in the heart of the backpacker district, this 3-star hotel has slightly higher standards than others in this price category. The rooftop restaurant-bar offers good views. Elios also has a gym, meeting rooms and lift.

Lavender Hotel $$ *208–210 Le Thanh Ton, tel: (08) 2222 8888, www.lavenderhotel.com.vn*. A much-needed new boutique hotel in this price category, the Lavender Hotel is already a firm favourite for its stylish, intimate ambience and great pricing. All rooms are nicely decorated and feature rain showers in the bathrooms.

Hotel Majestic $$$ *1 Dong Khoi, tel: (08) 3829 5517, www.majestic-saigon.com.vn*. This 1925-built historic landmark is one of Southeast Asia's classic colonial hotels. State-run, it still radiates old-world charm, with dapper bellboys, violin players serenading at afternoon tea and a grand marbled lobby with chandeliers and stained-glass skylights.

Hotel Metropole $$$ *148 Tran Hung Dao, tel: (08) 6295 8944, www. metropolesaigon.com*. The Metropole offers one of the most reliable and popular 3-star options in HCMC, plus friendly service. Features include gym, conference centre, small rooftop pool and snooker room.

Ordinary Bed and Breakfast $ *25 Dong Du, tel: 08 3824 8262, info@ordinaryvn.com*. The innovative creation of a Vietnamese-American owner-designer; it's anything but ordinary. This boutique hotel, within a narrow five-storey townhouse, seamlessly blends Indochina furnishings with modern comforts, like funky coffee bar and contemporary rooms.

Park Hyatt Saigon $$$ *2 Lam Son Square, tel: (08) 3824 1234, www. parkhyattsaigon.com*. With a vantage point overlooking the Municipal Theatre, this 5-star boasts some of the best service standards in Vietnam. The rooms feature colonial touches like four-poster beds and modern amenities such as rain showers and huge flat-screen TVs.

Renaissance Riverside Hotel Saigon $$$ *8-15 Ton Duc Thang, tel: (08) 3822 0033, www.renaissancehotels.com/sgnbr*. Located downtown along the river, this Marriott-managed 5-star offers high standards with a boutique-style vibe and exceptionally friendly service. Highlights include the 22nd-floor rooftop terrace pool, elegant 5th-floor Atrium Lounge and excellent Chinese restaurant.

Sheraton Saigon Hotel and Towers $$$ *88 Dong Khoi, tel: (08) 3827 2828, www.sheraton.com/Saigon*. The original 23-floor hotel with 371 rooms and suites has consistently been an award-winning favourite. Just adjoining it and opened in 2008, the 25-floor Grand Tower has 112 sophisticated studios and suites serviced by your very own personal butler.

Sofitel Plaza Saigon $$$ *17 Le Duan, tel: (08) 3824 1555, www. sofitelplazasaigon.com*. Opened in 1998, this remains one of the city's finest 5-star hotels. Stylish, contemporary flair extends from the stunning atrium-style lobby to the sleek rooms and suites. Facilities include rooftop pool, plus excellent fitness centre and ground-floor Martini bar.

NHA TRANG

Evason Ana Mandara $$$ *Beachside Tran Phu, tel: (058) 352 2811, www.sixsenses.com.* Nha Trang's most luxurious hotel, on a quiet stretch of beach. The attractive villas and suites have all mod cons as well as traditional touches such as ethnic minority tapestries. Two pools, tennis courts, a spa and two restaurants.

Jungle Beach $$ *Ocean Road, Ninh Phuoc Village, tel: (058) 362 2384, www.junglebeachvietnam.com.* This homestay resort is located on one of the nicest beaches in the country, one hour north of Nha Trang, at the Doc Let turn-off. The room rates include three meals per day and a free afternoon fruit salad. Jungle Beach is home to one of Vietnam's rarest primates: the black-shanked douc langur.

Mia Resort Nha Trang $$$ *Bai Dong, Cam Hai Dong, Cam Lam, Khanh Hoa Province. tel: (058) 398 9666, www.mianhatrang.com.* Mia is the newest edition to the Nha Trang Sailing Club resort-bar-restaurant-spa group. This luxurious eco-resort is located just south of the city on the way to Cam Ranh Bay, so its best to arrange transport (most likely from the airport in Cam Ranh) before you arrive.

Nha Trang Lodge $$$ *42 Tran Phu, tel: (058) 352 1500, www.nhatranglodge.com.* One of Nha Trang's biggest and fanciest hotels, with over 120 rooms in a high-rise tower that dominates the beach. Facilities include disco, business centre and restaurants.

Sao Mai Hotel $ *99 Nguyen Thien Thuat, tel: (058) 352 6412, email: saomai2ht@yahoo.com.* The large, tidy rooms at this friendly hotel have fans or air conditioning, hot water, a refrigerator and a TV. Sao Mai offers one of the cheapest motorbike rentals in town. All 20 rooms have balcony entrances.

Six Senses Ninh Van Bay $$$ *Ninh Van Bay, Ninh Hoa. tel: (058) 372 8222, www.sixsenses.com.* A favourite getaway of the rich and famous, this is perhaps Vietnam's most expensive resort, and certainly one of the most exclusive (white-sand Ninh Vanh Bay is only reachable by boat).

HUE

Century Riverside $$$ *49 Le Loi, tel: (054) 382 3391, www.centuryriversidehue.com.* Luxurious, grand hotel on the south bank of the Perfume River with comfortable rooms and a swimming pool.

Huong Giang $$$ *51 Le Loi, tel: (054) 382 2122, www.huonggianghotel.com.* Stylish hotel, with cosy rooms, pool and top-floor restaurant. Friendly staff.

Thanh Noi $$ *57 Dang Dung, tel: (054) 352 2478, www.thanhnoihotel.com.* Ideally located in the Citadel, within walking distance of the Imperial City, this place has character, budget rooms and a small pool.

HOI AN

The Nam Hai $$$ *Thon 1, Dien Duong Village, Cua Dai Beach, tel: (0510) 394 0000, www.ghmhotels.com.* This is easily Vietnam's most exclusive beach resort, with stratospheric prices to match. The smallest room is an oversized 80 sq metre (860 sq ft) villa.

Nhat Huy Hoang Hotel $ *58 Ba Trieu, tel: (0510) 386 1665.* Overall the best value in a city where accommodation is generally overpriced. This small, quiet hotel has friendly, English-speaking staff, and amenities that cost double the price at other hotels in town.

Victoria Hoi An Resort $$$ *Cua Dai Beach, tel: (0510) 392 7040, www.victoriahotels-asia.com.* Lying just 5km (3 miles) east of the town centre, this hotel has a fabulous private beach frontage and gorgeous rooms, with extra options, such as a pool and spa.

DALAT

Dreams Hotel $$ *Two locations at 151 and 164B Phan Dinh Phung, tel: (063) 383 3748, email: dreams@hcm.vnn.vn.* Luxurious, family-run, mini-hotel just north of the town centre. The rooms are well-equipped and have modern bathrooms. Generous free breakfasts and rooftop jacuzzi.

Hôtel du Parc $$$ *7 Tran Phu, tel: (063) 382 5777, www.hotelduparc. vn.* A slight step down from the Palace, this former Novotel is the second best accommodation in town and is within walking distance of the central market and the golf course.

Phuong Thanh $ *65 Truong Cong Dinh, tel: (063) 382 5097.* Located on a windy back street, this quiet hotel gives a great night's sleep. The tidy downstairs rooms in this family-run hotel have satellite TV and hot water. The central market is just a few hundred metres away.

Dalat Palace $$$ *12 Tran Phu, tel: (063) 382 5444, www.dalatpalace. vn.* Extensive renovations have restored this magnificent colonial-style hotel to its 1930s splendour. All rooms have fantastic views and are lavishly equipped. Drinks are served on the garden terrace, and there's a popular wine cellar bar.

MUI NE

Coco Beach Resort $$$ *58 Nguyen Dinh Chieu, tel: (062) 384 7111, www.cocobeach.net.* Coco Beach is Mui Ne's first resort and offers a tropical escape with no TVs in the rooms to help you focus more on the natural surroundings.

Joe's Garden Resort $$ *86 Nguyen Dinh Chieu, tel: (062) 384 7177, www.joescafegardenresort.com.* The seaside bungalows are equipped with minibars, free Wi-fi, porches with hammocks, and free breakfast.

Mai Am Guesthouse $$ *148 Nguyen Dinh Chieu, tel: (062) 384 7062, www.guesthousemaiam.com.* This Swiss-run mini beach resort is tidy and well kept. Each room has two beds, a safe, air conditioning and cable TV.

Mia Resort $$$ *24 Nguyen Dinh Chieu, tel: (062) 384 7440, www. miamuine.com.* Private bungalows hidden in secret tropical gardens at the re-christened Sailing Club. The beachside pool and bar is a popular hangout for guests, watersports enthusiasts and expats.

INDEX

Berlitz pocket guide

Vietnam

Third Edition 2013

Reprinted 2014

Written by Andrew Forbes and Ron Emmons
Updated by Adam Bray
Edited by Tom Le Bas
Picture Researcher: Lucy Johnston
Series Editor: Tom Stainer
Production: Tynan Dean, Linton Donaldson
and Rebeka Ellam

Photography credits

Cover picture: 4Corners Images

All photographs in this book by Peter
Stuckings/Apa Publications .

Every effort has been made to provide
accurate information in this publication,
but changes are inevitable. The publisher
cannot be responsible for any resulting
loss, inconvenience or injury.

Contact us

At Berlitz we strive to keep our guides as
accurate and up to date as possible, but if you
find anything that has changed, or if you have
any suggestions on ways to improve this guide,
then we would be delighted to hear from you.

Berlitz Publishing, PO Box 7910,
London SE1 1WE, England.
email: berlitz@apaguide.co.uk
www.insightguides.com/berlitz